"You Be Strong…"

My mother said.

MICHAEL TARULLI

First published by Busybird Publishing 2025

Copyright © 2025 Michael Tarulli

ISBN:
Paperback: 978-1-923501-29-4
Ebook: 978-1-923501-30-0

This work is copyright. Apart from any use permitted under the *Copyright Act 1968*, no part of this publication may be reproduced, stored in a retrieval system or transmitted in any form or by any means, electronic, mechanical, photocopying, recording or otherwise, without the prior written permission of Michael Tarulli.

The information in this book is based on the author's experiences and opinions. The author and publisher disclaim responsibility for any adverse consequences that may result from use of the information contained herein. Permission to use any external content has been sought by the author. Any breaches will be rectified in further editions of the book.

Cover Image: Elizabeth Richards
Author Image: Kim Landy
Cover design: Busybird Publishing
Layout and typesetting: Busybird Publishing

Busybird Publishing
2/118 Para Road
Montmorency, Victoria
Australia 3094
www.busybird.com.au

Readers are advised that some chapters contain graphic scenes of medical procedures.

I dedicate this book to mum and dad, for they endured my lived experience of tragedy, recovery, and re-emergence. I am forever grateful for their love and support.

To my dearest nieces, Carla, Bianca, Grace, Romi, Amelia and Sofia, and my nephew Gabriel, I hope I've instilled in you the wisdom and strength to be yourselves, to follow your dreams.

The high seas I sail, lost on waves of worthlessness

Legs unsteady, dampened hands, I clutch at the frayed rope

I am afraid and lost

The cold wind calls out, pulling me toward the dark abyss

I struggle free of its vortex and continue through the night

A tiny soul beneath a thousand stars, my friends for the evening

Led by the tides, I move with little resistance, resigning to the ocean's drift

Onward I journey to a destination unknown

Alas, I am a drifter

Michael Tarulli

June 2005

Contents

Prologue	i
I Will Not Die	1
Father Dillon	7
Dr Ritchie	16
Old Man	21
This secret between me and the tree	32
The Sound of Music	37
Leah	42
Caroline	56
UTI	60
Big Jim	65
Blowfly	71
Welfare	75
AIS	83
Shannon	88
Night Shift	91
Girls	94
Kev	96
Think of England	98
Taka	100
Floppy Eggplant	103
Do I belong here?	107
Home Again	111
Bad Moon Rising	117
Smoking	120
Crow Bar	124

"That's My Boy"	137
Wheels	143
Deep Blue	149
Yarran Dheran	155
Marta	163
A Pretender	181
Paesano	185
Man-Mountain Andy	188
The Quest to Walk	197
The Ultimate Challenge	200
European Summer	205
Purple Flesh	209
Tomorrow's Fish and Chip Paper	214
Senior Constable	220
Mr White	224
Call Me Tomorrow	230
No Better Than the Greyhounds	236
Man of Notorious Disposition	239
Love Letters and Poems	245
Bladder Reconstruction	249
New Beginnings	252
One Crutch	261
Lisa	264
"Be Strong"	268
Sakura	273
Reunion	283
Epilogue	288

Prologue

In 2017, two years after Mum had died of brain cancer, a community nurse named Emma visited the old home to discuss Dad's support needs. The conversation took place in the kitchen, where Mum, Dad and I had always spoken our truth. The care plan was progressing to my satisfaction until Dad interrupted to tell a favourite story, one he told over and over. He leaned forward in his chair toward Emma. "You know," he said, "Michael was the judo champion of Australia." A smile stretched across his face.

"Oh," she replied, nodding and smiling in acknowledgement, as one would to a child.

"Yes," I said, "that was many years ago now, Dad, when I was sixteen."

Emma turned and smiled at me. Dad's hearing was limited, and he didn't catch my words.

"He likes to tell that story. It's a distraction," I said to her with a wink.

She laughed.

Dad maintained eye contact with Emma, his striking blue eyes indication that he wanted to tell more. Once he caught her attention, he turned to me with sadness, and I feared what would come next. "He was fit and heldy, then he join de police," his voice cracked. A tear welled in his eye. "I never want him to join de police. I don't like guns. I remember the war," he shook his head, "horrible."

Then he told a story I had never heard before, of his wartime childhood in Italy. His eyes were fixed at a point behind me, in the far distance of the backyard. He was reflective and unmasked.

Dad's family had been forced to hide in a secret basement from the invading German army. Before all could settle, the family realised a younger brother was missing. Dad, being the eldest boy, took it upon himself to climb out of the basement to search and retrieve his brother, Furito, who was wandering outside their home. Dad picked him up in his arms and carried him to the bunker. Later, coming out of hiding, the family found their home torched to the ground. They learned of the rapes, and of the men who were roped by the wrists to horses and dragged away, never to be seen again. The surrounding hills were littered with guns and ammunition left behind by the raiders. As boys do, they picked up rifles and started shooting with live rounds; one local boy lost an eye from being shot in the face.

Dad concluded, "I didn't want him to join de police." He looked at me, "And... my boy got hurt."

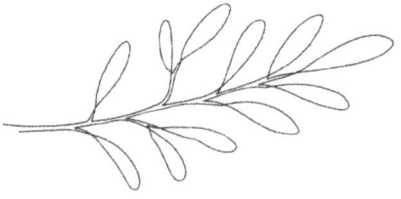

I Will Not Die

I was reborn on 16 April 1993. It was a Friday night. I was with my colleague Mark Moyle – senior to me by a year – on police duty in the Heidelberg area of Melbourne's northern suburbs. I didn't know Moyle very well, but he smelled of arrogance, this much I knew. We were on patrol at about 5pm when we received a call from D24 (radio dispatch).

"Shots fired at 326 Southbank Road."

"Heidelberg 206," I responded.

"Heidelberg 206, we have a report of shots fired in the vicinity of 326 Southbank Road."

"Roger that. En route, job number 27795."

The adrenaline kicked in as we drove to our destination. Moyle planted his foot on the accelerator and the car gathered momentum. The blue lights flashed, leading the way for us to own the road. My mouth clamped without voice. My mind seized without logic. My eyes were fixed on the street directory. The road was long and winding, and we were travelling fast. I raised my eyes as we reached a long, declining stretch of road to see a car entering from a side street, moving into our path. We approached the rear of the vehicle quickly. I felt as if Moyle was trying to tell the driver ahead to get out of our way.

My heart beat like a fist against my chest as another car entered the highway ahead of us. Moyle went to overtake it, but the driver moved aside to get out of our way and veered into our path. Moyle hit the brakes. My palms slammed against the door and the centre console as the Melways dropped to the floor. Moyle turned the steering wheel to his right as the car commenced sliding sideways with the tyres screaming against the bitumen. With the speed of a camera shutter, images froze one after another as our car headed toward the median strip. I gripped the "Jesus bar" above with my left hand, my right hand stretching out in front as if commanding the play to stop. My heart seized. I readied myself for the impact. The car first made contact with the roadside curb. I immediately felt like a hammer had struck my left hip. Intense pain shot from the base of my pelvis to the back of my skull. The car hit the steel guard rail, rattling my body. I felt like a smashed piñata as my fractured pelvic bones folded over one another. The pain hammered my pelvis like a blacksmith did his anvil.

My vision blurred from bubbles forming and bursting in my eyeballs. My ears buzzed a continuous monotone. The smell of burnt tyres and heated metal overwhelmed me. I sat on a mesh of bones, trapped in the crumpled cabin like wood in a carpenter's vice. When I finally managed to make sense of the world around me, I could see the road at a 45-degree angle to my left, and the centre console at chest height to my right. I pushed against the surrounding metal to lever my body free. "Get me the fuck out of here," I screamed. I turned to Moyle, who sat with his hands on his face, shaking. I yelled to lessen the pain, "Get me outta here."

"Shut up," Moyle pleaded. "I'll get help, just stop screaming."
FUCK YOU! I screamed inside. "AARGH."

He picked up the radio handset. "Heidelberg 206." His voice cracked, panicky. "In need of urgent assistance."

My lungs struggled to take in breaths, I felt like I was suffocating. The smell of fuel started to fill my nostrils. *I'm in so much trouble with Mum,* and with that thought came the memory of the wooden spoon breaking over my head when I was in strife as a child. *How crushed she will be to know of my fate.* I attempted to lift myself out of the car's grip, but my legs were too heavy and unwilling. I stared at them, my brain telling them to shift, but my black boots and uniform trousers failed to obey.

"I'm a doctor," said a man's voice. I looked over and saw a bearded man peering into Moyle's window.

Please! my mind yelled.

Moyle, with panic in his voice, shouted something at him.

I struggled to expand my lungs for much-needed oxygen. The clutch of childhood came to me, a judo contest, a schoolyard fight, all came back for one last round. Heat surged through my flesh, bursting at the skin like the boiled tomatoes Mum made for salsa in summer. I turned my head from left to right to left again, trying to shake off the pain. The collar of my shirt rubbed against my neck, causing it to feel like a knife cut.

My mind raced back to a job I attended where a teen had fallen off his motorbike on a highway. His shredded jeans revealed a severe laceration on his leg, the skin and muscle hanging off like jelly. Despite our efforts to restrict blood loss, he kept bleeding. His screams resurfaced and echoed in my head.

A sea of blue flashing lights flooded my vision as the cavalry arrived. The sound of the machine cutting the twisted steel that trapped me in its womb caught my attention. Then I thought of Mum again. I opened my eyes and saw the faces of young men in uniform beyond the broken windscreen. I focused on one young man with stripes on his sleeves. He was the closest, staring at me with a look of horror. I'm sure he would have pulled me out of the wreck if he could.

"Get me out of here," I screamed.

"Hang in there mate. We're here to get ya out," a man's voice yelled behind me.

The machine continued its song, cutting into, crunching and peeling the metal open like a tin can. I held on to hope, spurred on by both the stranger's voice and the machine.

"I can't move my legs," I yelled out, hoping the person behind would tell me differently. "Why can't I move my legs?"

"We'll get ya out soon, mate."

"Will I walk again?"

"We'll get ya out. Just hang in there."

I tilted my head back – "AARGH" – it seemed like an eternity. My body kept burning up, and my strength was falling away. I caught each ounce of oxygen with laboured effort. I felt death approaching. *No, I can't go now. I'm not ready to leave. I need to fight off this slip. I will not die.* "Please … I … can't."

"Hang in there mate," said the man behind me.

The night air began to invade my space as the steel can was pried open. A slight breeze flowed over my face and arms, soothing my fiery skin.

"Just going to give you something for the pain," a soft voice called out.

My arms remained rigid; hands pressed hard against the slanted roof.

The man grabbed my forearm. "Relax your arm."

I let go as instructed. He inserted a needle into my vein. The liquid ice snaked its way along my blood vessels, cooling the burning sensation. I remained awake, though I let go of my fight. As the drug took effect, my body slumped like an inflatable tube man at a car yard.

I was finally freed and hoisted aloft by my rescuers. I was on a high, riding under the Milky Way as I stared into the night sky, watching the beautiful stars dance.

This wasn't the first time I had been delivered from a car in an emergency. On a cold morning in 1967, outside Box Hill Hospital, I emerged from the back seat of the neighbour's car with the help of Mum and the doctor.

The story goes that I started moving early. Mum alerted Dad, who in turn alerted the young couple next door, Richard and Mary. Richard drove Mum and Dad to the hospital as I made my way down Mum's uterine wall. The car stopped short of the hospital's entrance. I was delivered at 5:05 am on 10 May.

"You very quick Michal," Mum said of my sudden arrival.

I was transferred to the ambulance. Flat on my back, I stared into a white haze, the wailing siren and rushed voices filled my ears.

"Hang in there, Michael," a man's voice kept repeating.

I trusted the people who were with me. I arrived at triage; the lights above blurred out by the flurry of arms and hands like a movie projector gone wrong. I resigned from the conscious fight and surrendered to the strangers in masks.

I recall my brother Marcello stating years later, "The car was unrecognisable." He recounted the state of the vehicle from the news footage of the accident. He said I was trapped for over an hour. I haemorrhaged from severed blood vessels between muscles and splintered bones. At the hospital, Mum had sat slumped in the adjoining room, hearing my pained cries from the emergency room. Mirella, my sister, held blood bags under her top to warm them in preparation for a blood transfusion. I was fighting for my life.

Father Dillon

I opened my eyes. It appeared to be the next day, or maybe a few days after; I lost sense of time. The dark room, the Intensive Care Unit, had become a living tomb as I woke in and out of a dream.

Senior Sergeant Howe, the commander of Heidelberg Police, with his familiar thick moustache, stood holding his police hat close to his chest. Wayne Keough, a friend and colleague at Heidelberg Police, stood next to him. He had lost all his colour, including his freckles.

"G'day, young fella," Howe said, trying his best to smile.

I raised my hand to acknowledge him. A nurse approached; her body pressed over me, adjusting the intravenous line. Her angelic face gave a gentle smile of reassurance. Howe raised his eyebrows in a flash. I gave a thumbs-up, which drew his laugh. I had no idea of the severity of my injuries; the drugs were most likely making me happy.

Moyle stepped out from behind Howe, his face revealing an anguish. "Sorry mate," he said.

I tried to tell him I was alright. The nurse approached with a chalkboard, guiding my hand as I wrote, "I'm ok."

Moyle turned away, burying his face in the palms of his hands.

I opened my eyes to find Mum, Dad, Marcello and Mirella by my bedside. I couldn't speak so I waved my hand to say hi. The hammering of nails into fragile bones meant little in comparison to the sight of my family's anguish.

As a child, I was drowned out by the booming voices of the family during evening meals. I repeated my protestations and opinions thinking they were not heard the first time, but eventually fell silent among the clattering voices. Here, I found myself the centre of attention.

Mum held my hand tight, trying to put on a brave face. "Michelangelo," she said, brushing her fingers softly against my face. Dad looked worn and weary.

"I'm sorry," I tried telling them both.

Mum turned to the nurse, "What he say?"

I tried again, my mouth opening and closing like a goldfish. The nurse brought over the chalkboard, and with her guidance wrote, "I'm sorry."

"*Oh, figlio mio* (Oh my son)." She leaned over and kissed my forehead.

Mirella held my hand.

I wrote like a fifth grader, "Don't worry. I'm ok." I thought I'd be out of the hospital in a week or two.

"Yes, Michael," Mirella said, nodding her head in approval. "You're doing ok."

I wrote on the chalkboard with Mirella's help, "My gym membership?" I paused before regaining enough strength to continue. "Suspend it." I handed the board to Mirella.

She read the message and turned to face me. The inner corners of her eyebrows were raised, and the corners of her lips were pulled down. "I'll let them know," she said.

I turned to Marcello, who offered a sad, tired smile. I wanted the familiar expressions of laughter and madness reminiscent of our young days.

Once, when an old relative from Dad's side of the family had passed, Marcello and I were with the gathered mourners, standing at the burial site as the priest delivered his final prayer for mercy. I nudged Marcello to look in the direction of a colossus nearby who sported heavy-set sideburns and deep-set dark eyes.

I leaned close to Marcello and said under my breath, "Doesn't he look a lot like Andre the Giant?"

We tried to contain ourselves out of respect for the bereaved, but our mouths were writhing to conceal the laughter inside. The harder we fought it, the worse it got – we both had tears flowing down our faces.

Dad turned to us with an inquisitive look. He could have mistaken our behaviour for weeping.

The nurse came over and whispered in Mirella's ear.

"We're going now, Michael," Mirella said, kissing my cheek. "See you soon."

Marcello clasped my hand, "See you, Michael."

"Bye, Michal," Dad said, fighting off tears.

Mum leaned over and kissed my forehead, "Ok, Michal?"

I nodded in reply. Her soft hands stroked the length of my arm. She left my side to join the others.

I tried to call out, "Please don't leave." As the door closed behind them, the machines became noticeable again, "Berdup berdup, b, bip." The blackness returned; creatures of childhood nightmares emerged from the shadows in my sleep; they'd sneak up and slide in next to me. I felt them breathing over my neck, their weight bearing down on me; they'd stare into my very soul. I was too weak to fight them off, and I'd wake in severe sweats with trembling hands. I cried like a child, taking small breaths so as not to be heard by the nurses. The feeling brought back the memory of when Mum let go of my hand on the first day of prep school; I was alone and afraid.

I suffered continuous bleeding from pulmonary contusions and damaged capillaries in the lungs. A tube was inserted down my throat and into the trachea to clear the excess blood, causing my heart to arrest. The surgeons attempted to restart the muscle with the defibrillator, but my heart refused to react. They split my sternum apart with a sternal saw, opening layers of skin, tendon, bone and muscle. The retractors exposed my heart for the surgeon to hand pump. He did this at a rate of approximately 100 beats per minute to keep my body from dying. The procedure of "butterflying" my chest and hand pumping my heart over and over was repeated for days.

The family was called to the hospital, keeping a bedside vigil, watching me continue the fight, the rib cage lifting and dropping in a wave-like motion, capturing oxygen to fuel vital organs.

"He has a two-to-five per cent chance of surviving through

the night," the surgeon said to Mirella. "We are going for one last attempt to stop the bleeding. It's up to Michael now." Tubes were inserted into the trachea and sides of my chest to drain the excess fluid from my lungs.

Dad could barely see through swollen eyes, wiping away tears with his handkerchief.

"Mum," Mirella said, "If Michael dies, I will give birth to a son like him."

"No one can take the place of Michael!" Marcello cried.

"What you think?" Mum said, "You think you can make another boy like Michal? No." She shook her head, "Only one Michal here."

She collapsed to the floor and, leaning on her elbow, looked up to the heavens, tears flowing down her cheeks. "Please, not take Michal. Madonna, per favore." She buried her head into her forearm, "No, no, no."

Mirella and Marcello wrapped their arms around her shoulders, helping her to a chair.

One day, or night, in my near-death state, I had a surreal experience. I floated on my back. There was no sound. The light shimmered, its source neither the sun nor artificial means. A faceless, naked woman approached me from behind. She wrapped her arms around my chest in a loving embrace. My head rested against her soft breasts. Backwards, we drifted gracefully. Backwards, we drifted in the swirl of water, in the stream of a rainbow ride. She gently placed the palm of her hand onto my forehead, the side of her face pressed against the back of my head.

She whispered, "Don't be afraid, you are safe with me." Overwhelming love flowed through me as I continued this carousel of endless bliss.

I opened my heavy eyelids; the magic moment was gone. I became confused about my environment: the sound of alarms and a chorus of voices filled my ears, the sight of surgeons wearing masks and hair nets was before me.
"It's going to be ok, Michael," a woman's voice said.
"Where's the naked lady?"
She looked at her colleague, who looked down at me.
"Michael," she said, adjusting the IV line. "You're going to be ok."

I told my friend, Chris Haggarty, of my encounter with the naked lady. He replied, "I'm not surprised, even at the hour of death you would come up with some erotic fantasy to play over in your head."

As a student at Aquinas Secondary College, I hadn't expected to develop a kindred friendship with Chris Haggarty. One day, in year 8, I saw Chris doubled over with arms raised, protecting himself against repeated blows from Squiz, a third-rate bully.
"Oi, leave him alone," I yelled.
Chris looked at me with a helpless expression of relief.
Squiz turned and scurried off with his shoulders slouched, yelling, "Shit a brick. All's good, Mick."
We found solace in our shared experiences. He was made fun of for his size, and I struggled with the tag of "wog" – the title removed my Australian identity, even though I made the

footy team at school, played cricket with my neighbours, the Hepburn boys, and loved eating Four'n Twenty pies with sauce dripping down my fingers. The one thing I admired about Chris was his sharp wit.

"Hey, Haggas," Squiz yelled to Chris, "Did ya have 'haggis' this morning?"

Chris's baby face blushed. "Didn't take ya medication this morning, I see," he called back.

I became more aware of my surroundings over time. My flesh took the form of a concrete slab with an electric current running through it. Desperate for the sensation to stop, I drifted in and out of sleep.

I opened my eyes to find Chris sitting beside me, his face pale.

"G'day mate," he said in a low voice.

I lacked the energy to say hello back. He knew my discomfort. I pulled the sheets off my chest as the heat had become too much. I set my eyes on the staples that stretched like a zipper from the top of my sternum down to the diaphragm. I glanced back at Chris, with a look that said, "What the fuck happened here?"

"It's ok mate," he said, stroking my hand with his clammy hand. "They had to stop the bleeding in your lungs."

For whatever reason, I didn't want him holding my hand.

The incision reminded me of the shrieking swine at the mercy of my uncle's blade – Christmas in Italy, 1978. Like a surgeon, he ran the blade from throat to underbelly; the innards spilled out, steaming. My aunty, holding the bucket beneath, caught the entrails. The smell of warm blood left a metallic taste in my mouth. I pretended to be unmoved, cringing inside. I had become that violated carcass.

I got the nurse to help me write on the chalkboard for Chris to read.

"Look after my mum and dad," I scrawled.

"I will, mate."

I awoke to see a Doogie Howser lookalike working away with a tiny spanner at the metalwork designed to repair my shattered pelvis. The apparatus looked much like the Eiffel Tower, rising above my abdomen. I didn't know what purpose it served at the time; I just knew it was a part of my body. Drops of sweat ran down the sides of my chest as the vice-like clamp squeezed against my bones. He paused to adjust his glasses and looked up. My eyes said it all, the "piss off and leave me" stare. He moved on without a word. I lowered my head to the pillow and drifted into a deep sleep.

The next time I woke, I found Father Dillon standing in a cassock, splashing holy water over my face. I blinked to deflect the drops from my eyes. He smelled of old wooden pews, bringing back memories of my days at church. He performed the sign of the cross with a prayer book in hand.

Aren't the last rites reserved for the dying?

"Hi, young man," he said.

I tried smiling to offer false gratitude. His presence brought back the vulnerability of my youth, a sickly feeling. The younger me who listened to Father Kevin Dillon's sermons on a Sunday, wearing my crucifix with pride, was no longer the same person before him.

I remember I was in my first year at Aquinas Secondary College in 1980, I ran to St John's Church every Sunday for mass with the gold crucifix bouncing off my chest; the necklace was a gift from Mum. I arrived to a full house. Father Dillon watched my every step; I walked to an empty seat, believing he was disappointed in me for turning up late. I sat down in the last pew, catching my breath, drained by the heat and shame. Having received holy communion, I walked back to my seat and knelt. The wooden pew pressed hard on my knees as I prayed, trying to free the stale bread stuck to my palate. "God, help Mum and Dad get along without arguing, and forgive me for saying 'fuck' the other day."

I imagine if I had been raised in the old country, Italy, the birthplace of my parents, the town elders would've groomed me to a life of celibacy in the clergy.

"Think of your recovery like the Melbourne Marathon," Father Dillon chuckled. He was aware of my running achievements in cross country and athletics, representing Aquinas College at inter-school competitions.

He held the rosary beads. "You'd be in Seaford by now," he smirked.

I forced a smile in response.

"Well, I'll get going." He nodded his head. "I'll see you next week."

I lifted a hand to signal my gratitude for his visit and watched him walk out of the room.

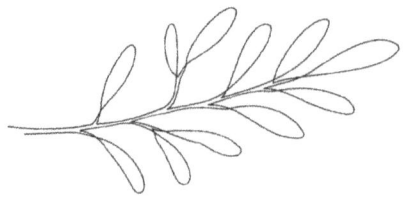

Dr Ritchie

About a week after Father Dillon's visit, a doctor with a bushy moustache walked up to the side of my bed. "Hi, my name is Dr Ritchie," he said, smiling. "I'm the surgeon who operated on you when you came in." He scanned the length of my body. "You realise you're a lucky man?"

I nodded my head for the sake of agreeing with him.

He walked to the end of my bed. "How are you feeling?"

I gave a nod of the head to indicate I was doing ok.

"I thought of you over the weekend, wondering how you were doing," he said, holding onto the bed frame with outstretched arms. "I took the family to the beach house. I told my wife about you. You worried me, young man. We almost lost you."

A sickly feeling rose from my stomach to my throat. I stared at him, dumbfounded. I had no voice.

He walked and stood beside me. "I'm glad you're on the mend," he said, placing a hand on my shoulder.

I felt awkward, thinking I owed him a debt for saving me. He smiled and tapped my shoulder before walking off. I returned my attention to where I lay, stiff as a wooden plank on an air-inflated mattress. I was turned every two hours to avoid pressure sores from developing on my hips, heels and tailbone. My face sank into the pillow, back to the familiar sickly smell of latex, replaying his words: lucky – had me worried – almost lost you. I thought about his casual manner, as if he had said, "Meh, you nearly carked it."

I was facing a photo collage pinned to the wall, the light above highlighted the faces of family and friends. I reached out with an effort to touch the laminated prints, going as far as an inch or two. Further up the wall hung a poster from the football club I played for, Box Hill Mustangs, with the get-well messages written in black by each player. I didn't care much about any of these. I closed my eyes, remembering winter days of eating Chiko rolls at the footy, of summer holidays catching cicadas from the bark of gum trees and clasping the legs of crabs in rock pools by the beach.

The symphony of electronic equipment continued its melody, "Berdup berdup, bip, bip," serving as a distraction from the pain. The interplay of sounds reminded me of Yazoo's "Only You", evoking feelings of love and youth. The intravenous lines, like wires on a power pole, draped over my torso, arms and neck. The tracheostomy tube kept the windpipe open to aid my breathing and clear mucus. The sensation was like a spiked cricket ball stuck in my throat, which made swallowing painful. The dialysis machine served as an artificial kidney, removing waste and extra fluid from the blood. The infusion pump provided liquid nutrients and pain relief. I looked up and settled my eyes on the helium balloons – "Get Well", they read. I detested them because they symbolised the divide between my entrapment and those free to walk.

All that came before – what made me – had been taken away; my thoughts trapped in a hollow cage. W*hy me? What have I done to deserve this?* I scratched my head and stared at the ceiling light above, looking for answers. I scratched my arm close to the intravenous site, feeling the bony point of my elbow. I twisted my arm around and noticed the outline of my bones, the years of built-up muscle had wasted away. Both arms were thin as matchsticks. I hadn't imagined the God I grew up with would treat me like this. *Was I living in sin that he punished me for? Was it because I drifted away from him? Was he pulling me back in again to teach me a lesson?*

I'd been in the ICU for about a month when the tracheostomy tube was removed. It was just in time for a visit from Mum.

"Hi Mum." I sounded like Freddy Krueger. "Happy Mother's Day." I waited for her reaction as she held my hand.

"*Cosa vuoi dire* (What do you want to say)?" She turned to the nurse, "What he say?"

I tried again, "Happy Mother's Day."

"I no understand him."

The head nurse, more like a headmistress, instructed me to repeat the words. "Michael, say it louder and clearer, go on," she said, standing with hands on hips.

"Happy … Mother's … Day."

"Oh, *figlio mio*," Mum held my hand to her chest, leaned over and placed a kiss on my cheek, holding back the tears. "Good, Michelangelo, good."

"Here, have some ice cubes, Michael," the head nurse said, shaking a cup with the clinking sound of ice. "This will soothe your throat."

I moved the cubes around with my tongue to hasten the melt. The liquid worked its way down my gut. The icy treat eased the dry burning sensation of the mucus lining – it was better than ice-cream.

About a week later the dialysis machine was no longer required. Chris told me that he had observed Dr Ritchie shout "Yes!" and perform a fist pump as a result. The bean-shaped organs had begun to function on their own.

About two days later, I began breathing exercises to develop my inspiratory muscle strength. The physiotherapist, who looked like she'd come straight out of high school, visited me daily, encouraging me to clear my lungs.

I did as she demonstrated, breathing in and huffing forcefully, bringing up phlegm from the little air sacs, much like the sound of a cat coughing up a hairball. Each day my lungs breathed deeper and stronger.

I opened my eyes to see Father Dillon standing beside me once again.

"Hi young fella, how are you today?" he said, trying to look upbeat.

"Hello, Father," I said with a hoarse voice.

"Sorry I'm late, I attended a funeral this morning. The third one this week, can you believe?" He put on his stole.

Sheesh, you know how to cheer a bloke up, Father.

"One must be prepared for the unexpected," he said, opening his prayer book. "In the name of the Father…"

I stared at the illuminated exit sign as he continued his prayer.

I felt uncomfortable. My memory took me back to when I was a churchgoer, and the vulnerability of young Michael at Aquinas College. My student reports typically read: Michael is very well-liked by fellow students. He is very popular, has a good sense of humour, and mixes well with his peers. Little did they know of my fragile interior, a heart of glass prone to fracturing. At lunch break I'd walk along a stony footpath behind thick shrubbery, looking around to see if anyone noticed me. I'd open the chapel door slowly; the creak of the hinges would cut the sound of silence. I'd peer inside, walk in light-footed and sit on a chair against the back wall. I'd take a deep breath and exhale, allowing my shoulders to slump forward. The stillness came to life: wattlebirds clucked in the garden, brushing their wings against the leaves as they jumped from branch to branch, and the buzzing sound of a blowfly could be heard near an open window that let in the distant sound of students in the schoolyard. The sunlight peered through the leadlight window, casting colours onto the carpeted floor as I dug the thumbnail into the palm of my hand. The swell of emotion lifted from my stomach to my throat. The bloodied and sorrowful Jesus nailed to the wooden cross looked down on me. I stared at him. *How do I get through the day? I'm afraid.*

"... In the name of the Father, and of the Son, and the Holy Spirit, Amen."

I felt compelled to reply. "Thank you, Father."

He closed his book and took off his stole. "You'll be in Seaford by now," he smirked.

I didn't have the heart to tell him he'd said the same last week and the week before that. *Surely, after a month, I would've moved on from Seaford.*

Old Man

It was early June.
"Would you like to go outside, Michael?" the nurse asked, "There is a barbeque fundraiser for the hospital, in the courtyard."

I looked at Mum and Dad. They reminded me of kids waiting for a parent's reply. I nodded my head. The nurses wheeled my bed outside the ICU, my nerves a combination of excitement and dread.

"You ok?" Mum asked, holding my hand.

I nodded. The bed thudded against the door flaps, and I continued along the corridor and down the elevator. The external doors released the automated locking mechanism. As soon as I exited the sun pressed its heat on my face; the cool breeze flowed over my eyebrows and lips. The smell of burgers over a gas barbeque invaded my nasal passages. The high-pitched sound of children's voices reminded me of the St John's Fete, where, as a child, I'd meet up with my "girlfriend", holding her hand on the mini train named Stanley. A tear formed in the corner of my eye. When you've experienced near death, somehow the slightest of memories find their way into your heart.

Dad's smile was a welcome sight, the same smile he carried when he took Marcello and me to the Royal Melbourne Show when we were kids. I heard a trumpeter and a banjo player performing "When The Saints Go Marching In". I looked around but couldn't see them. Mum held onto my hand while Dad made duck squawks to the children running past; they stopped to listen and laughed with him. A familiar face approached me, I recognised his cheesy grin and large frame.

"G'day Michael," he said, extending his hand to shake mine.

I smiled, "G'day mate."

It was Craig Kelly, the centre halfback for the Collingwood Football Club. I recounted to him the story of when I stopped his car in traffic for an illegal turn at a city intersection.

"You wound down your window and said, 'Officer, I just wanna get through, traffic's banked up the other way.' And I said, 'Ok, only coz I'm a Collingwood supporter.' And you said, 'Thanks mate.'"

"I remember that time," he laughed.

On reflection, I doubted he remembered.

"Thanks for letting me through." He turned to his assistant, who handed him a rolled-up poster. "Here mate," he said, scribbling on it, "For you to keep by your bedside." He handed me a black-and-white Magpies poster with the message: *All the very best to you Michael* and ending with his signature, *Craig Kelly*.

I smiled like a kid again.

"He's my son," Dad chipped in. "He's a champion." Dad's grin was broad as the face of Luna Park.

Kelly shook Dad's hand, "And a proud father you are."

As soon as he departed, another identity approached. Greg Evans, the television show host of *Perfect Match*.

"Hello, my name is Greg Evans," he said, shaking my hand. "And what's your name?"

"His name is Michal," Mum said, delighted to be in his company. She enjoyed watching him on TV.

"Hello, Michael," he smiled just like a gameshow host, "Are you enjoying yourself today?"

I nodded my head, staring at his shiny teeth, neatly styled hair, and tanned skin. *So, this is what they look like up close.*

"Are the nurses treating you well, Michael?"

"Yes," I answered, mesmerised by his appearance. *How does he keep his teeth so white?*

Mum couldn't contain her excitement. "I see you on *Perfect Match*."

I was glad to see her smile.

"You... very funny."

"Oh, thank you," Greg replied.

"And the machine. I like him too."

"Oh, Dexter." He laughed. "He's a troublemaker."

How does he keep his skin so tanned?

"You get well young man," he said, shaking my hand before walking away.

The smell of burning sausages, the yelling of kids, the continuous banging of cymbals and the trumpet screech all became too much. My vision began to blur, my world began to spin around me.

"Mum, Dad, I want to go back now."

The next morning, I was awoken by a familiar voice.

"Good morning, young man."

I opened my eyes to see Dr Ritchie sporting a cheesy grin. He had company; gentlemen smartly dressed in suits who looked at me like bug-eyed parrots.

"I brought some friends along," he said.

I nodded in acknowledgement.

"We're going to perform a test to see if you can feel the point of this needle." He held up a threading needle, like the one Mum used to sew the buttons on my shirts with. "Tell me if you can feel the point against your skin. Can you feel this?"

I shook my head.

"How about here?"

"No."

"Can you feel the needlepoint now?"

I waited for a pressure point. Dr Ritchie pricked my toes, the soles of my feet, the top of my feet.

"Can you feel any pressure?" he said, looking at me.

I pressed my hand against my forehead, "No."

He stood up and tweaked his moustache. "Ok, I'm going to apply pressure to the back of your calves." He looked up, "Can you feel this?"

"No." I gave the same response when he applied it to the front of my lower legs.

"Ok", he took a deep breath. "Now I'm going to apply the pressure to your upper legs." He lifted the bedsheet, exposing my thighs. "I'm going to press the needle on your upper legs. Can you feel anything?"

"Yes."

"What can you feel?"

"I feel a tingling sensation," I said with an exasperated breath.

"How about now?" The point of the needle was now placed on the side of my left leg.

"Yes, I can feel that."

"On a scale of 1 to 5, 5 being the strongest, how would you rate the pressure applied?"

"Feels like a 2."

"Ok." He threw back the bedsheet. "We'll leave you alone now," he said, placing his hand on my shoulder. They left as they arrived, like ghouls. I suspected the diagnosis wasn't good.

I was transferred to the spinal ward, an upgrade from the ICU. I became conscious of my surroundings like a prisoner bordered by four white walls. The routine became all too familiar: the orderlies arrived to lift and turn me every two hours; doctors did the morning rounds with their pens and clipboards to check me over; cleaners came by with their mops smelling of bleach, never raising their eyes from the floor; the kitchen staff delivered meals on plastic trays, morning, lunch and dinner. Stale urine and the two-hour post-poo smell were sickly reminders of my time as a student nurse. The profession I once trained for came back to haunt me, and as luck would have it I was on the receiving end.

    I shared my room with three older men. My saving grace was the location of my bed, parked next to a window in full view of a tall gum tree standing proudly among the surrounding shrubs. He reminded me of the giant ghost-white gum in our neighbour's front yard, who I named Old Man. As a child, I pressed my forehead against the windowpane, counting the branches hanging off the trunk. From a teen with braces to a young man finding his way into the world, I sought Old Man's advice from my bedroom window. On most occasions, I took heed of his guidance.

I returned my attention to the gum tree on the hospital grounds. I rested my eyes on the outer leaves and followed the line of its inner branches to the large trunk. *What a splendid spirit you are.* I visualised the roots extending below the surface, reaching out to occupy a large portion of the earth. *The roots run deep with this one.* He spoke to me of strength, for he exemplified it. He provided comfort to my weary body, serving as a distraction from where I rested.

Each day Mum walked kilometres from the Sidchrome factory where she worked to be at my bedside. She would turn up at half-past four in the afternoon, straight after the *Bugs Bunny Show*. She covered 3 kilometres of walking, as she did all those years ago, from the Stanley factory to our home in Mitcham. She wore her blue uniform with the familiar factory odour I remembered as a child, greeting me with a kiss on the cheek. She looked exhausted at each visit, which worried me.

"Ma, it's too far for you to walk. Don't do this, please."

"Tsk, no worry about me," she said, rubbing the back of my hand.

"But I don't want you to be tired. It's too much for you."

"If I work, and walk every day, it make me strong. Strong for you, Michal."

I was reminded of the day when I sat in my fiery-orange 1977 Holden Gemini, waiting for Mum to exit the door from the four o'clock knock-off at Stanley. It was summer, December 1988; the north wind brought the desert heat with it. I turned up the volume listening to Australian Crawl's "Errol", tapping the dashboard and singing along with the chorus. A police car pulled up in front, parking near Nunawading police station. I remembered sitting on the policeman's motorcycle as a child during a school excursion out the front of this building. A senior officer stepped out of the car wearing silver pips on his shoulders. He placed a cap on his head, sliding his fingers between the bridge of his nose and its peak. He was tall, sturdy and muscular, an officer of prestige and power. The sound of the car door handle jolted my senses back to normality.

"Hi, Michal," Mum said with a deep sigh, sitting with her hand pressed on her forehead.

I kissed her on the cheek, "Hi, Ma." Her face was hot from working under a corrugated iron roof, operating a mechanical metal cutter.

"*Che caldo fa* (How hot is it)?"

The smell of machine oil clung to her dark blue uniform.

"How was work, Mum?"

"Tsk, ok."

I sensed her internal pain developing as I drove home, hoping her daily bath would do away with her troubled mood. I became used to her silence; her mind was elsewhere. After her wash, she took to her favourite armchair and reclined to face the ceiling. The dark cloud remained with her, exaggerated by the extending creases of her forehead. I walked over and began to rub her shoulders from behind. "It's ok, Mum, you can relax now" (I remembered Nonno Joe's instructions back in Italy: *look after your mother*). I saddled on the armrest beside her and gently massaged her head, focusing on the temple region. Her head flopped about like a rag doll.

"Like making pasta, hey, Ma?"

She opened her eyes. "Squeeze da brains out, Michal, please."

I laughed at her retort, and she followed, laughing out loud. I held her tight around the shoulders. I thought it was now or never. I'd been hanging on for too long. "Mum… I want to join the Police Force."

She looked up with a furrowed brow. "What?"

"I want to be a policeman."

"Tsk!" she said, looking at me strangely. Her reaction was conveying a message of doubt. I'd hoped for a positive response. Mum closed her eyes and laid back to rest. I walked to the corner of the room and sat down on the rough carpet. I put on the headphones and listened to EON FM, watching the clouds morph into shapes, like the underside of ocean waves breaking on the shore. The rumbling storm announced its presence as raindrops hit the windowpane. They struck harder as the grey set in. I planted my forehead against the glass, feeling the drops rattle against my skull. Old Man gum tree stared at me from across the neighbour's property, thrashing its limbs with the wind. The radio announcer introduced the next track, "Here's one of my favourites from The Doors, 'Riders on The Storm'." I closed my eyes and started singing under my breath, *"Riders on the storm... riders on the storm... into this house we're born... into this world we're thrown..."*

Dad arrived by my bedside an hour later than Mum. His workplace, the Camberwell Council depot, was further away. His overalls wore the dirt from the trenches he dug on roadsides and nature strips. I believe they insisted on continuing to work to cope with their suffering, and both watched me with tired eyes.

Dad sat to my right, lifting my drainage tube to aid the flow of urine from my bladder to the silicon bag hanging off the edge of the bed. Mum stood to my left, massaging my legs and feet, whispering under her breath; a silent prayer, I imagined. It was painful to watch Mum perform this ritual. I withheld the urge to tell her to stop. I knew this was her way of coping with private grief.

All my life I've known both my parents to be tireless workers, doing hard labour at their respective day jobs. Both arrived as migrants from Italy, seeking a better life and fortune. Mum arrived in 1960, alone, without knowing a word of English. Her father paid for her voyage to the great southern land. Dad arrived earlier, in 1953; half of his family had established themselves in Fitzroy. Mum and Dad were introduced through acquaintances. Mum told me how she was struck by his handsome looks. "Tsk, he good looking," she said, raising her eyebrows and staring off into the distance. She proceeded to tell the story of how Dad tried to kiss her on their first date, to which she pulled away, and struck him on the nose with a fork. "Not until we're married," she said. I laughed upon hearing this, imagining the stoic tone in her voice. Within six months, they were married, 30 December 1961.

I tried to conceal the pulsing pain. To speak of it would've broken them both. I imagined the devil standing over me, jabbing me with his electrically charged pitchfork. He'd prod, short and sharp, at the soles and heels of my feet, morning and night. He'd impale the length of my legs, promising never to leave me. I gripped the sheets ever so tight as the pain came and went in waves. I couldn't hide it; they knew.

I looked at Mum, "Don't worry."

"It's ok, Michal," Mum said, continuing to rub my feet.

I turned to Dad. My concern for him weighed heavily. I scratched my forehead, "How was work today, Dad?" He shrugged his shoulders with a look of deep sadness.

"It's ok, Dad," I said, reassuringly.

I insisted they needn't come every day after work, preferring them to go home and get some rest instead.

The truth was I needed time alone.

My hips went from purple bulge to pale skin against bone. My heels and coccyx peeled open like onion layers, revealing the reddened dermis underneath. I lay on my left side, stiff as a board; every two hours, I was turned side to side to keep off the affected area to allow for healing. The clock's hands pointed to 10 o'clock. I gripped the soiled sheets between my fingers, twisting the ends around my hand. The smell of my grown hair mixed with head sweat became nauseating. I heard footsteps and laughter from the corridor. The orderlies' arrival came as a relief.

"G'day, Mike," said Steve, drawing the curtain around my bed.

"Boys," I said, nodding my head in acknowledgement.

"Time to move over to your right, yeah?"

"Whatever you say, boss, just don't drop me."

"Not if Geoff can help it, he had a few beers last night at the Old England."

"Oh, shit. I'm gonna be dropped."

A chorus of laughter erupted. "Nah, you're right with me, Mike," Geoff said, "it's Steve you've got to watch out for."

Steve shook his head at Geoff, "How many did you have again?... Ok, on my orders, one, two, three and lift."

I twisted in the air like a corkscrew. The bones cracked in my lower back. I felt the unnatural pressure of metal pins deep inside my pelvis.

"Rowan, ya meant to follow Geoff with the turn," Steve called out.

"I did, but Geoff stepped to his left."

"No, I didn't."

"Geoff you stuffed up," Andre intervened.

"You right, Mike?" Steve asked.

I composed myself from laughing. "Yeah, mate, all good."

They tightened the fresh bedsheets, fluffed the pillows (one was used as a hug pillow) and tucked me in. I can imagine how comforting adult hands are to infants, the warmth and security of being wrapped up in blankets.

"See you in a couple of hours, Mike."

They walked off into the dark, continuing with their bickering. The pain in my right hip increased as I watched the minute hand make its way around the clock. The sheets began to soil again. The pillow gathered head sweat and the smell of latex became strong. In the dark, I lay still, unable to sleep, waiting for their return like a child in need of his mother.

This secret between me and the tree

A gentleman wearing a suit and tie walked into the room with a nurse trailing behind. It was the morning rounds for doctors. He greeted my fellow roommates by their names; I guessed he was the doctor in charge of the ward. His eyes locked onto me from behind thick-framed glasses.

"Hi Michael, I'm Dr Wu, the spinal ward specialist. How are you feeling?" He appeared to be a cheerful man.

"I'm ok."

"Good, good." He pressed the middle frame of his glasses. "You're a policeman, right?"

I felt sick from the exposure and the anticipated follow-up questions. "Yes."

He had that look of, "Shit, what happened to you sucks, hey?"

I stared at him blankly, not wanting to continue.

"Ok," he said, grabbing his necktie. "You need to eat. Maybe have a meat pie with a pint of Guinness?" he joked. "You need to put on weight."

I hadn't realised how gaunt I'd become until I looked at myself in a handheld mirror to shave. My cheekbones and chin were prominent, and the orbital bones were clearly outlined. My nose appeared larger than I was used to.

I was looking forward to eating my first meal, for I relied on nutrients via the intravenous line since admission. My first meal was lunch – a triangular sliced sandwich with ham and cranberry sauce. It was no match for the mortadella and provolone rolls I was used to eating before the crash. For dinner, I sipped on the disgusting dishwater they called mulligatawny soup and nibbled at the tuna mornay. The following morning, I ate toast with Vegemite, and lunch was the Australian version of lasagna – cardboard pasta sheets with dodgy mince.

That night, my small intestines began to work after a two-month hiatus. What commenced with cramping developed into excruciating pain. It felt as though a living creature with sharp claws was working its way along my intestinal tract. I resisted pressing the call button so as not to disturb the nurses. I fixed my attention on live Test Cricket from Old Trafford, England. The claws dug in harder. I tried to double over, only to be restricted by the pelvic rods. "Arggh, fuck," I cried out. I pressed the buzzer long and hard.

"Yes?" A nurse with a soft voice approached; her name badge read "Veronica". She turned off the call light, "What seems to be the problem?"

"My guts are killin' me." I looked at her with desperation, "The pain's getting worse, like someone's stabbing me in the guts."

"I'll give you something to lessen the pain."

The wait for her return seemed longer than I anticipated.

"Here," she said, offering me the pills and water. I swallowed the white-coated compounds and reached out for her tiny hand. "Fuck, it hurts."

"It will soon pass," she said.

I looked up, "Please, kill me now." I squeezed her hand tight.

Veronica rubbed my hand as a mother would with a sick child, her sympathetic eyes watching over me.

A euphoric shout from the sports commentator caught my attention, another Shane Warne wicket, dismissing an Englishman. The replay distracted me from the pain for a second. I held Veronica's hand tighter as the steely claws dug in further along the intestinal tract.

"It'll be ok, the pain will soon pass."

The strain of the previous night carried over into the morning. I awoke to the sound of clattering dishes from a moving trolley. I wiped the gunk build-up in the corner of my eyes.

"Good morning," the kitchen lady said, "Your breakfast is here." She placed the tray beside me. The smell of burnt bacon and eggs filled my nostrils. I lifted the silver lid from the plate; the meal looked stale. I reached for the orange juice, tore off the plastic seal, and slowly sipped on the nectar.

"Good morning," Dr Ritchie said, walking in front of my view of the garden. "Something smells nice."

"Hi, Doctor." He seemed too casual for my liking. Something wasn't right; I could feel it.

"How are you?"

"I'm ok." I held the napkin tight around my fingers.

He took a deep breath. "Michael, there's been no improvement with you over the last month or so." He paused to rub his moustache. "Michael… you'll never walk again."

What did you say?

My chest caved in, hit by a sledgehammer. His face was deadpan, without emotion, "You'll become dependent on a wheelchair."

I stared at him, overwhelmed with numbness. I wrapped the napkin tighter around my fingers.

"The good thing, I guess, is that you can still work in the Police Force, maybe become a detective?" He tried his best to be upbeat with a smile. "You'd wear nice suits as they do in the movies." He was one step away as I dug my thumbnail into the palm of my hand. The silence made us strangers. "Ok!" he said, tapping the bed frame with his hands, "I'll leave you to enjoy your breakfast."

I felt the shadow's presence over my shoulder. I stared through the window at the garden as the wound in me swelled. The emotional outpour started as a trickle and became a steady flow of tears. I placed my forearm over my eyes. The interior wall broke down, piece by piece, leaving nothing but a vacuum.

Chris Haggarty came to visit not long after, as if fate had willed it to be. "You right, mate?" he asked, placing a hand on my shoulder.

I informed him of the prognosis, repeating Dr Ritchie's words – "You'll never walk again."

Chris's face turned scarlet red, his eyes suggested helplessness.

I waited for him to breathe, let alone talk.

"Michael, I'm gonna kick your arse to make ya walk, if I have to."

I wasn't sure whether to laugh or cry at the remark, considering there wasn't much of my buttock to kick. I wiped away the tears and let out a deep breath. "I want to be left alone," I said, staring ahead.

"Ok, mate." He held my hand. "I'll see you after work… ok?"

I nodded in acknowledgement. He walked away as I returned my gaze to the window. I set my eyes on my friend, the gum tree, standing white and grey in the mist. Birds jumped from branch to branch. The leaves were ever so green. I followed the branches to the large trunk, and visualised the roots extending below the surface. I called out to the old gum tree; *How I admire your stillness. You are humble and majestic, not a worry in the world. Remove me from here and make me part of you, to become the roots beneath you, where I can hide from the earth above.*

I developed a strange feeling as though someone had pressed the factory reset button. This feeling drew me back to my younger years, when I struggled with my place in the world. I reflected on when I was at my strongest, the judo years. I was full of vitality, training after school, running kilometres on roads and hills around Donvale and Mitcham, in preparation for the state and national tournaments. Taka, my sensei, would ruffle my hair or place his hand on my shoulder, his gesture of congratulating me on winning first place. *If I could reach out to him, what would he say to me right now?* I knew the answer, he'd encourage me to fight on, no matter what.

I remained lost in the space of my being, lying on my side, absorbing the sensory chaos plaguing my body; pain saturated my flesh. I tightened my face and made a fist to embrace the will to fight on, for a ball of fiery hope mushroomed from my midriff.

Sometime after my discharge from the hospital, I wrote the following poem about my determination to walk again:

> The tree, Old Man, spoke to me like a friend. Only me and the tree. My new friend and me. The seed had been planted; defiance grew within, knowing deep down I would walk again. This secret between me and the tree, I would walk again.

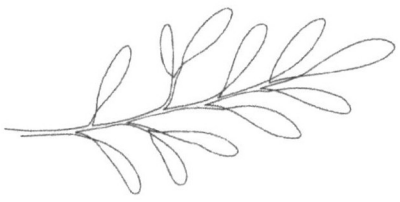

The Sound of Music

A deep-sounding voice snapped in the air, startling me awake. "Hello, my name is Anja. I'm your nurse today." Her accent suggested she was from Russia. She was tall and built like Xena, the warrior princess. "I will give you a suppository."

I tensed upon hearing the word suppository. As a nurse in training, administering a suppository into a patient's rectum was one task I couldn't stomach, and now I was on the receiving end of one.

"Are you ready?"

Do I have a choice?

She pulled the screen curtain to shield off prying eyes, lifted the bed sheets below my waist, and then my gown. I stretched my neck to watch her put on latex gloves and smear lubricant on the end of her finger.

"Relax," she said.

I laid my head on the pillow with my eyes closed. I felt something forcing its way into the rectum.

"Are you relaxing?" she said, pushing the suppository further up.

I wouldn't know if I was. I clenched my teeth and gripped the bedsheets as a warm feeling erupted in my colon.

"I'll come back in fifteen minutes, ok?"

I nodded nervously and waited for my dormant bowels to wake up and do their work.

Fifteen minutes passed.

"How did you go? Did you empty?" Anja lifted the bedsheets and turned up my gown.

I waited for a reaction.

"Nothing," she mumbled, dropping the sheets over me. "I'll come back in fifteen minutes."

Another fifteen minutes passed with the same result, I hadn't emptied my bowels. Then another fifteen minutes before Anja gave up, muttering in her native language. I had disappointed her.

Much like my bowel movements, I had always moved at a tortoise's pace. My mind and body were slow to mature compared to my peers – I reached puberty late, and I lost my virginity later than my male peers. I hid under my shell for years, afraid to stray outside the boundary of piety; unlike my peers, I refrained from swearing, smoking and drinking.

Unlike Mirella and Marcello, who relished their youth, I was the opposite, preferring the safety of home life. I often wondered whether I was a genetic mistake. A year younger than me, Marcello stepped out on a Friday and Saturday night to meet with his mates or go on a date with a new girlfriend, which I envied from afar. Instead, I had Bill Collins entertaining me with his *Golden Years of Hollywood*. I witnessed the night's remnants the following morning with the overpowering smell of beer from Marcello's side of the bedroom.

Marcello hadn't suffered the same torment at school as I did. He was popular among his peers. Mirella was three years older and a regular night owl with her hangout sisters. She, too, was popular among her friends.

The orderlies arrived hours later, in the afternoon.

"G'day Mike, time for a turnover."

"No worries," I said, eager to relieve the pain.

"Ah, change the sheets, boys," Steve said.

My embarrassment spilt over as the smell became obvious. "Sorry guys."

"Not to worry, Mike," said Geoff. "Steve doesn't mind little surprises now and then." A chorus of laughter erupted, much to my relief.

The news of my diagnosis reached Mum and Dad before I spoke the words. Their sadness heaped over me like wet cement. We didn't talk about the doctor's sentence, that I would never walk again. I looked Mum in the eye to offer reassurance.

"Mum, I'm strong, don't worry," I said with a sturdy tone, making sure Dad heard me. He was seated with his head bowed.

"Ok, Michelangelo," she replied, caressing my hand.

Dad hardly raised his eyes to meet mine. He lowered his head, brooding as he watched the urine trickle into the bag with his hands clasped on his lap.

"I'm ok, don't worry."

The longer they remained, the harder it became for them, watching on like I was a helpless infant. I tried my best to mask the emotional pain. Dad shed tears, and glanced upward to the heavens. "Oh God," he said, baring his teeth in anger. He wasn't a religious man, but on this occasion he was.

"Dad, please," I said with exasperation. "I'm ok. I'm strong." I wanted order to be restored, to go back to the way I remembered us on a calm Saturday night – Dad reading the *Il Globo* in the comfort of his chair, and Mum enjoying *The Sound of Music*.

I remember laying prone facing the television, my elbows resting on the carpet, hands propped under my chin, watching *The Sound of Music*. I swore it had aired on television months earlier. Bill Collins gave his glowing endorsement of the film. Mum leant forward in her chair as Julie Andrews pranced around singing, "these are a few of my favourite things". Dad, on the other hand, sat in his chair reading the *Il Globo* newspaper, far more interested in the internal mayhem of Italian politics.

"What's going on in the mafia world, Dad?"

He pulled the corner of the paper away and lifted his reading glasses. "What?"

"What's happening in the mafia world? Like, who killed who?" I smiled, raising my eyebrows.

"Tsk," he remarked, turning back to reading the obituaries. The Gambinos of the world mattered not to him; it was his beloved Abruzzo that defined his Italy. His description of Cansano, his birthplace, sounded like a Monet painting; his smile widened as he spoke about it. He penned a rhyming poem in Italian which in part read:

> Cansano, the jewel among the sea of bright yellow globe flowers spread over fields in spring. The beautiful mountains in the background, sprinkled white before the winter snow covered them.

"What she say, Michal?" Mum asked about the lyrics Maria Von Trapp was singing. I tried in my best Itanglish to explain the Do-Re-Mi bit.

"Look, it's just a silly song Mum, *tutti pazzi* (they're all mad)."

She laughed at my retort.

"Mum, *vuoi un cazzo di caffè?*" I confused the word *tazza* with *cazzo*. Instead of asking, "You want a cup of coffee?" I had said, "You want a fuck'n coffee?"

"Oh Michal," she said, throwing her head back in hysterics. "You de only one who make me laugh."

Dad pulled the newspaper back, staring at Mum with curiosity.

I was brought back to the present by Mum rubbing the back of my hand. "It's ok Michal," she repeated, nodding her head at me. "It's ok."

Leah

In the quiet moments, I counted the number of pinholes in each square tile of the ceiling. Some tiles were marked by water stains that made images: *that's a mouse smoking a pipe, that's a woman's lips shaped to be kissed, or is it a baboon's butt?*

The silence of my dormant state was broken by a steady influx of family and friends. I answered the same daily questions with the same daily answers.

"How are you today?"

"Yeah, I'm ok."

"You feel any better?"

"Yeah."

"What did the doctor say today?"

I'd shrug my shoulders, "Nothing's changed."

I cringed whenever a familiar face walked into the room. Not because I disliked them – I didn't want to be seen in a state of vulnerability. One day, my grandparents from Dad's side walked in a slow procession, searching me out among the strange faces that greeted them. Nonno, with his fedora hat and suit, and Nonna, with her floral headscarf and winter shawl wrapped around her shoulders, caught sight of me. My heart seized momentarily. They shed tears. Nonno took off his hat and Nonna sniffled at her tissue. I held their hands firmly. We didn't say much, there was no need.

I recall visiting their home in Mitcham every Friday afternoon on my way home from school. Nonna's smile was a welcome relief from the schoolyard dystopia.

"Michelangelo," she'd say cheerily. "*Oh figlio mio, accedere* (Oh my son, come in!)."

The familiar smell of home-cooked pasta sauce and sight of timber décor greeted me. I was treated with a cup of milk and sweet biscuits, or peeled apples and sliced oranges. Nonno was a quiet man. I never knew him to speak English, so I did my best to converse in Italian, only to falter. He laughed at my attempt to pronounce the words correctly.

"*Ho bisogno* (I need)," he said, using his hands to accentuate the word.

I repeated the word, "*O... biz...ono.*"

He laughed, composed himself, and repeated the words "*Ho bisogno.*"

I replied, "*Si, certo* (Yes, of course)," using my hand to emphasise my delivery, which had him in hysterics.

In hospital I would offer a tired smile and fake laugh to keep visitors entertained – to make their visit worthwhile. The presence of Mum and Dad helped relieve the discomfort, diverting attention away from me, up to the point when Dad spilt his testimony. "Michael is number one," he said, with assertiveness. The look on his face showed his determination to repeat the words. "Yep, number one."

Uncles, aunts and friends would nod in agreement to appease his suffering. My face would colour each time he said it. It reminded me of the time he informed the principal of Aquinas College, Mr J Arthur, of my success at the national judo championships in 1983.

Mr Arthur, a former boxer turned principal, entered the classroom. "Excuse me Mr Reece, mind if I have a minute with the class," he said in his familiar deep tone. Mr Reece, our room teacher, stepped aside.

Mr Arthur turned to face the class, "Good afternoon, boys."

"Good afternoon, Mr Arthur," we all replied.

"I have good news to share," he said, playing with the pen between his fingers. "One of our students won the under-16 national judo championships last weekend."

I froze, sitting on my chair with heat coursing through my body.

He smiled at me, revealing the white of his teeth behind his beard, "You've done our school proud, Michael Tarully." He, like everyone else, pronounced my surname to rhyme with Scully or Tully.

My name is Tarulli, like Tabouli.

"Let's give him a round of applause."

The class turned their attention toward me and applauded.

"Onya, Mick," I heard someone yell, and, "Good stuff, Micky T," from another.

I figured Dad had informed Mr Arthur of my achievement. I imagined him bursting into his office to announce the news, a proud father moment.

I felt a craving for rest, removal from the visitors, and a moment's peace with my friend the gum tree. The winter added colour to his mood; silent and at peace. That's what I was yearning for, time alone with my friend.

"Good morning," the nurse called, drawing the window curtains back. There wasn't much good about it. The fog sat low, obscuring the view of the garden. I could just make out the shape of the old gum tree, grey, standing there like a ghost. Comforting to know that in the coldest and darkest moments, Old Man was there for me.

Moments later, Moyle's girlfriend Sarah arrived, bearing a bouquet. "Hi Mick, I brought you these to brighten your day."

I first knew Sarah when she was engaged to a friend of mine, who I worked with at City Patrol. When I arrived at Heidelberg I learned that Moyle had left his girlfriend to be with her. Not hard to believe. Sarah was petite, attractive and smiled like an air stewardess. And Moyle could win over a girl with his hypnotic charm.

Police members from Heidelberg were on strict orders not to visit me in hospital, except Wayne Keough, who I had requested to be the sole representative to see me and who was a conduit of support to the family.

I felt colour and heat wash over my face; surprised by Sarah's presence yet delighted to be the focus of her attention. "Oh, thanks."

"I'll get you a vase for these." She returned from the nurse's station with a vase. "So, how are you feeling?" She asked, arranging the coloured blooms.

"I'm doing ok. But the food is terrible!"

"Yeah, not the same as homemade meals, hey?"

"Nah," I threw my head back on the pillow, "and I could kill for a chicken and chips from Donny's." There was an uncomfortable gap in the conversation "How's Wayne?"

She sat down on the chair facing me. "Wayne Keough," she said, raising her eyebrows. "Yeah, he's ok, I think." She hesitated. "I hardly see him, we're on different shifts."

"Say hi to him for me?"

"I will."

I tapped away at the overhang bar.

"Have they given you a time when you can go home, Mick?"

"No, I don't know how long I'll be in here, to be honest."

She fidgeted with her fingers, and her smile disappeared. Her lips crept with nervousness. "Hey, have you been interviewed by the AIS?"

The Accident Investigation Squad. A sickly feeling stirred in my gut and my mood started to turn. "Not yet."

"What are you going to tell the investigators?"

I grasped the overhead bar and lifted myself onto my right elbow. I could feel the muscles in my forehead tense. "I don't think it's wise to talk about it, Sarah."

"You know it wasn't his fault, don't you?"

I paused, sick to the core. "I don't want to talk about it."

"It was just an accident. No one was at fault."

"You can leave now."

She stood up. "It wasn't his fault," she protested. She smiled like she was unbothered, but nervous all the same. "I'm just saying."

I watched her walk away. The thought struck me with intense anger – *I'm the one who's bleeding here, not your beloved Mark.*

That night, in my hot head, I played over Sarah and Mark Moyle discussing what I'd tell the investigators, whether I'd testify against Moyle's driving on the night of the accident. I was angry. I pictured them coming up with a scheme to cast doubt on my version of events. My imaginings were broken by Veronica's flashlight moving about as she approached my bedside.

"Michael, a young lady is waiting outside for you," she whispered. "It's Leah, she wants to see you."

"Ok."

"She can't stay too long, it's after hours."

I nodded.

My heart began to beat fast as a dark figure approached my bed. Leah's face came into view under the bed light. I smiled with a sense of unease.

"Hello, my love," she said. Her sorrowful face was on show. She reached out and latched onto my hand. "How are you?" she whispered.

"I'm ok."

"Are you in pain?"

I scratched my forehead, thrown into a feeling of a stranger, unsure how to proceed. "A little bit."

She shuffled the chair closer toward me, "I'm thinking of you always." The familiar smell of her perfume, the same one she wore when we were together, came rushing at me. It was a welcome break from the hospital smell I had become accustomed to. She caressed my hand, "Is there anything I can do for you?"

I looked over at the tray table, "Can you please pass me the glass of water?" I took a sip of the water, contemplating whether to detail my injuries to fill the silence. "I may have to have a skin graft over my coccyx; there's a hole developing there." I lifted the catheter and the drainage bag attached to it, "My bladder has a catheter hanging off it to empty the urine into this bag." I took in a deep breath and exhaled.

"Can you move your legs?"

The question brought on a brittleness that threatened my masculinity. "I can't," I whispered, shaking my head. "I can't move my feet or legs." The intravenous machine beeped loudly through our pauses. I could hear my heart thumping against my chest. "I can't feel anything below my waist."

Leah slid her hand underneath the sheets, beneath the bridge of metalwork. "Can you feel that?" She asked, brushing her hand along my inner thighs.

"Sort of; it's like a tingling sensation."

Her fingers worked on exciting the phallus. "Can you feel that?"

The memories of our lovemaking came to the fore. We were reminiscing about a past love.

"I can feel it… but it's not like before."

Remembering our time together hurt me more than the lack of feeling in my body: *if only it were possible to roll back time.* I carried a heavy burden; the breakup with Leah stained my mind, the guilt spilling over. I gripped her hand tight. "Sorry, I didn't mean to hurt you."

"Shh, it's ok. Just get better," she said, caressing my hand.

I turned and looked up at the ceiling. The unease began to lift. I wanted the attention diverted from me. "So, what have you been up to?"

Leah spoke about the movies she'd seen at the cinemas, the inventive meals she made for dinner, what her family and friends were up to…

I nodded off and woke up again. "Sorry," I said, shaking my head to keep awake.

"I'll go now." She leaned over and kissed my forehead, "Bye, my love." And with that, she disappeared into the dark. I wondered if that was the last I'd see of her.

Dr Wu entered the room for the morning rounds. "Good morning," he said, adjusting his spectacles.

"Hi." I was nervous. I looked at the interns and nurses standing aside with their pens at the ready. I swallowed and looked him in the eye, "Can I ask you a question?"

"Depends on the question," he said with a chuckle.

"Will I get my sexual function back, like… have a normal erection?"

He touched the bridge of his nose where his glasses sat. "Michael, you have damaged your spinal cord and sacrum. You have lost the ability to have an erection, ok?" The look he gave indicated he wanted me to agree with him.

"Yes, but I can feel some stimulation down there."

"You suffered so much trauma, Michael… the sexual nerves from the sacral area leading to the penis are damaged," he said, demonstrating the anatomy with his hands.

Veronica looked at me, her eyes telling no lie. She saw the emptiness in my expression. If she felt empathy, she didn't show it.

"Ok?" He tapped my shoulder as a sign of encouragement.

The medical team moved on to the next patient, leaving me to reflect on my half-a-man condition.

I was hoping he would tell me differently, that my erections would go back to normal, give it a year or two. My conscience toiled away with deep regret at not making the most of my sexual opportunities in my younger days. I thought about missed chances, the "should've done this" and "should've done that." Fantasy overtook reality like a runaway train. *Why didn't I ask her out when I had the chance? Why didn't I fight for her? Why didn't I react when she showed interest in me?*

I was denied a sex life in the prime of my manhood. I reflected on my nursing days in 1988 and the time I was tasked to write an essay on human anatomy for my first assignment. I scoured the library's bookshelves for research materials on human physiology. A book about the reproductive system caught my interest. I read a chapter about erectile dysfunction due to trauma, where excited signals to the corpus cavernosum to sustain an erection were impeded. A cross-sectional diagram of the penis and its damaged sacral nerves heightened my anxiety. *What if that happened to me?* I knew it was irrational, but the thought terrified me at the time. I stared at this diagram for longer than necessary. And now that harrowing fear had become a reality. I struggled to convince myself that this was an unfortunate accident and not a punishment from God.

My view of the world became smaller; visitors, doctors, nurses, cleaners, and kitchen staff, were all I knew.

I turned to view my friend the gum tree. The strong wind forced his head to sway back and forth, the branches rising and falling as if in a dance. *Maybe Old Man is just as wild and confused as I am.*

I imagined if I stared at him long enough, he'd provide some glimmer of hope and comfort to this lonely state of being.

Don and Josie, Chris Haggarty's parents, came to visit me one Saturday night. I was prepared for their arrival, having been informed by Chris earlier that day.

"G'day Mick," Don said, shaking my hand vigorously. I never knew him without a smile.

"How are ya, Mick?" Josie said with her usual stoic tone, not revealing too much of her sorrow. She greeted me in the same manner as always. Whenever I visited the Haggarty home, I'd find Josie seated in her chair by the fireplace. "G'day, Mick. How are ya?" she'd ask, insinuating I needed help.

"I'm good thanks, Mrs Haggarty." I always answered, "I'm good," even when I wasn't.

Don looked for a chair to sit on. "Not mush…room here, Mick?" He said, giggling.

"Oh, Don. Zip it," Josie retorted.

I shook my head, remembering the old days with Don's old jokes. "She'll be right, mate," and "fair dinkum" were familiar phrases in the Haggarty household. I was at a Haggarty barbeque once when Don asked me to "pass the dead horse" for his burger. I handed over the salt, which was apparently referred to as Harold Holt.

"Nah, mate," Chris's younger brother, Marty, said. "The tomato sauce."

"What's the to-mato with you?" Don quipped, chuckling to himself.

Don wiped his nose with a handkerchief. "Father Dillon sends his best, Mick."

"Ok, how is he?"

"He's good Mick, still collecting from us poor parishioners," he laughed.

"The choir still going?"

"They no longer have a choir, Mick, haven't for years," Josie said.

"Hey, Mick, remember our footy trip up at Yea?" Don smiled. "Big Mick [Dad] and your Uncle Fury [Fiorito] cooking spaghetti in that big pot?"

"I do remember."

"Oh, you kids loved it."

I smiled at the memory of Dad stirring the large pot, the vapour rising as kids watched on, licking their lips. I wasn't sure who had more fun, Dad forking the spaghetti and dishing it up, or the boys gleefully watching the pasta fall into their bowls.

"I taught you how to play footy. You know that right, Mick?" Don said with a grin.

I never knew if he was joking or if he meant it. I smiled at him, nevertheless.

To pass the time, I'd watch daytime television – soap operas like *Days of Our Lives* and *The Bold and the Beautiful*. Mirella brought me an anatomy book to colour: it included muscle groups, the bones of the skeletal system, and major arteries and blood vessels. I had pencils of various colours to fill the spaces between the lines – red, blue and green. The orderlies handed me a selection of adult magazines, hidden in large envelopes.

Yet the scenery outside was far more interesting. One day, a crow landed on my friend. I kept watch on him, suspended high on a branch, turning his head in all directions as if he were looking for an audience. He took the action of squawking, lunging forward with an extended neck and open beak. I couldn't hear his call. *Stay there, don't you dare move.* The sun illuminated his black feathers, giving off a glossy shine. He turned his head left to right to left. *You are handsome. I wish for the freedom you have, a free spirit. Where is your home?* I imagined trading places with him and flying away from this chaos.

"Michael," a voice called out. I turned to see Veronica approaching. "You have very important visitors, by the look of it," she said with enthusiasm. I held onto the overhang bar and propped myself up on my elbow. In full regalia, the Assistant Commissioner walked into the room, baring his teeth in a smile like a dodgy car salesman. A nervousness overcame me, like a kid whose ball had gone over into the angry neighbour's yard.

His driver, a lanky Senior Constable, followed behind. Patients and visitors watched him parade with long, even strides. I had the feeling he was enjoying the attention.

"Good morning, Mr Tarully," he said, shaking my hand to prove his strength. "My name is Brian Bishop, Assistant Commissioner."

My name is Tarulli, like Tabouli.

"Sir." My facial muscles tensed on hearing his name. *God isn't letting me go too easily.*

"The Chief Commissioner extends his regards and well wishes."

I twisted the bed sheet around my index finger.

"So, how are you today, young fella?"

"I'm not too bad, thanks, Sir."

"Are the nurses looking after you?"

"Yes, they are, Sir."

"Good to know." He took off his hat. "You have the support of Police Command." He was too clean-shaven to be taken seriously, without even a blemish. "If you need anything, just let me know."

"Yes, Sir."

"Know that your family are looked after."

This remark triggered a nerve. I didn't want the police to bother Mum and Dad. They were hurting and I could imagine they would want to be left alone. I recalled Chris Haggarty telling me of an encounter Mum had with Senior Sergeant Howe shortly after the accident – he hadn't been forthcoming with responses to her demands about how the accident happened, or who was responsible. I imagined her Neapolitan rage expressed through steely eyes and flared nostrils. Wayne Keough had become the intermediary between my parents and the police since. I felt the need to protect my parents.

"Police Welfare are in contact with them," Bishop continued.

I knew Wayne was there for them.

"You'll be out of here in no time," Bishop said, rocking back and forth on his feet, clasping his hat.

"Yeah, I guess," I said, trying my best to sound jovial. The driver never said a word. I looked at him, wondering how he came to be his driver. The moment's silence made for an uncomfortable exchange.

"Is there anything you need, young fella? Anything at all?"

"No, I'm okay for now."

"As I said, if you need anything, let me know." He smiled again. "This is my number." He handed me his business card. "Don't hesitate to call."

I nodded in acknowledgement.

"We'll look after ya."

What exactly did "look after me" imply? I thought. We were strangers, and I became far removed, at will.

He placed his hat back on his head. "Take care, young fella." He shook my hand to end the meeting. A weight lifted from my shoulders as I watched them walk away.

Veronica approached minutes after they left. "Well, how did the meeting go with your police friend?" she asked with a smile.

I looked away. "Oh, yeah, it was okay," I said, scratching my nose.

To the police department, I was Constable 27795, just a number. To Mum and Dad, I was their son.

Caroline

I was pleased to see Veronica on the morning shift. "Ok, now for the blood pressure. Relax your arm," she said, wrapping the cuff around my arm. She inflated the cuff until the nylon stitching was tight around my humerus, the pressure squeezing against the muscles and bone.

I looked into her eyes. Veronica reminded me of Caroline, the girl I had a crush on at Aquinas College. Veronica had striking blue eyes and short blonde hair, like Caroline, but more than this, she had the same sweet and sincere demeanour.

I remembered the first time I met Caroline. From years seven to ten, Aquinas College was split into two campuses, an all-boys school and an all-girls school. The two campuses were separated by a recreational space where liaisons between the sexes played out during lunch breaks, under the watchful eyes of teachers. The senior school, years eleven and twelve, was co-educational. I only had chance encounters with Caroline at school; my heart leapt at the sight of her each morning walk to school. I looked forward to seeing her again as the bell sounded to end the day.

One day, Caroline approached me as I walked off the oval alone after an inter-school football game. She wore her school blazer and woollen scarf. "Hey, Mick," she said, brushing her blonde hair behind her ears.

"Hi." I struggled to meet her gaze. My stomach fluttered with nervous excitement each time I caught her soft blue eyes.

She scanned me from head to toe. "Look at you. You're soaked."

I looked down at my waterlogged jumper, hanging off like a poncho. "Yeah, it was muddy down there."

She laughed. "Did ya win?"

"Yeah, we won."

"Your sister's name is Mirella, right?" asked Caroline

"Yeah?"

"Well, my sister Maree and Mirella are good friends."

"Ok. I didn't know that." I did know, but didn't let on.

"She's nice, your sister. She's told me a lot about you."

I felt my face turn red. "Ok." I scratched my neck. "Well, I gotta go and get changed," I said, pointing to the clubroom with my thumb.

"Ok, see ya, Mick."

I raised my hand to wave, "See ya."

Veronica released the air pressure from the cuff. "You're due for a clean, mister." She handed me a cup of water to take a green oval-shaped antidepressant pill. "I'll come back in half an hour."

I was always itching, from head to abdomen. The grimy sheets clung to my sweat; its prickly fabric irritated the skin with every slight movement of my able body parts. The inability to scratch the itch tested my endurance. I lifted the bedsheet to relieve the irritation. I looked down at my frail and twisted naked body. I noticed, for the first time, the contorted shape of my pelvis. I dropped the sheet and ran my hands over both sides of my pelvis. *Yes, my left side is lower than my right.* As the bruises and swelling dissipated, the skeletal form took shape in contrast.

Veronica returned, holding a wash bowl with warm, soapy water. "Now for a wash, young man." I watched her as she placed the wash bowl onto the tray and drew the curtain around my bed.

As she lifted the sheets, I blurted out, "My hips are out of shape."

Veronica wrung the washcloth. The smell of fragrant soap hit my olfactory senses.

"Why aren't my hips even?" I wanted her to understand that my physical appearance was important to me. "I don't like the lower hip on my left."

She stared into my eyes and drew a deep breath. "Well, you sustained so much damage, Michael. You shattered your bones." She paused. "The surgeons did their best to reconstruct your pelvis."

I felt a hollowness as if my soul had been ripped out. Veronica carefully removed the gauze attached to the skin against the metal fixtures. The smell of betadine and skin decay became noticeable. I gripped the sheets as she cleaned each site with the dampened cloth.

"Can they reconstruct my pelvis? I'd like them to operate on me to set my pelvis even."

She stopped. "Michael, you're lucky to be alive. They did their best to repair you."

I refused to take in her rationale.

"And you've got a skinny bottom, which didn't help."

So, I am guilty of having a skinny arse. And like Humpty Dumpty, I was put back together again in an odd-shaped way.

Dr Wu entered the room for his daily morning round.

Oh great, here we go again.

"Good morning, Michael," He adjusted his thick-framed glasses. "I understand you are concerned about your pelvis?" he said, wide-eyed. I felt embarrassed by the revelation.

"Yeah, I noticed my pelvis is not even." I lifted my bedsheet and looked at my lower half to emphasise the point. "The left is much lower than the right side."

"Michael, you came to us with severe trauma." He stared at me. "You shattered your pelvis. I've seen your X-rays and CT scans. The surgeons did their best to reconstruct the pelvis."

I took a deep swallow, "Can they re-operate on my pelvis, like, break it again and make it even?"

He shook his head, "Michael, that is not an option. Your pelvis cracked like an eggshell." His voice was rising to emphasise a point. "Consider yourself lucky, if you were a female, you wouldn't be able to bear children," he said with a chuckle.

What an odd thing to say. Fuck you!

"Ok." He scratched his neck, "I'd better let you rest." The team walked away, and I was left to stew in misery.

I have endless X-rays, CT scans and MRIs, enough to fill a library shelf. The images of my pelvis disturb me; like a Picasso cubist painting, the left sitting bones appear lopsided compared to their counterparts. Closer inspection reveals jagged edges and tiny fragments bound together like a jigsaw puzzle. The lumbar vertebrae show cracks. The sacrum is unrecognisable.

UTI

It was a Sunday afternoon. Mum and Dad brought the steel pot with the broken handle and the white bowl with ornate edging; a reminder of home. Dad lifted the lid from the pot as the smell of onion, garlic and herbs circled me. Mum carefully ladled the *zuppeta* (soup) into the bowl while Dad took ownership of spoon-feeding me. I allowed him to do so, knowing he received satisfaction from feeding his boy. The taste of softened celery, beans, and broken pasta went down well with the broth. As I received each spoonful, he'd mimic my open mouth; I hadn't swallowed before another spoonful appeared at the ready. I stared Dad in the eye. I was a slow eater and didn't want to be rushed. He ignored my displeasure.

Mum spoke up. "Michele, *fai piano* (take it slowly with him)."

I felt my stomach churn, on the edge of rejecting the homemade goodness. The room started to sway as I tilted to one side. Sweat beads ran down my chest, and I felt a flush cross my forehead before bringing up the meal. Each heave of my gut brought on the sharp pain of metal constricting my mending bones. And after each heave, I thought of Dad, how he'd be crushed inside to see this.

"I'm sorry, Mum," I said, frustrated after having thrown up again. I had brought up rogan josh the previous day, splashing it over the bedsheets like watercolour.

Dad, holding the bowl, raised his eyes to the heavens and shook his head with clenched teeth. I'd seen that expression of rage before, when I was in trouble as a kid. He lowered his head, "Fuck'n," he murmured. I shared his frustration, but kept quiet. His anger turned to despair as tears trickled down his cheeks.

Mum approached me, composed, holding in her hand a damp cloth, and placed it over my burning forehead. "It's ok, Michelangelo," she said, caressing my cheek with her soft hand. The memory came to me of being a child in bed with a sore throat and constant cough, and Mum placing a damp cloth on my forehead and rubbing my chest with ointments.

"I'll be right," I said, looking at the two, my arm extending out to reach for their hands.

The next day, Nurse Erica placed her soft hand over my wrist. "I can't feel your pulse, are you alive?"

I am now, I thought, admiring her Mediterranean brown eyes.

"I'm going to take your blood," she said.

I watched as she put on gloves and attached the needle to a syringe.

"Just a little sting," she said, working it into my thin, wasted arm. A few blood droplets resulted from each attempt. "I might try your other arm." She tried again and again. "It doesn't appear I'm having much luck."

Though the sensation was like an ice pick digging into my flesh, I remained silent.

"Sorry, sweetie," she said.

"That's ok," I said, feeling brave.

"There we go." She turned to me and smiled as blood filled the syringe. "Now, let's have a look at your urine." She picked up the drainage bag. White cloud-like formations floated down the plastic tube from my suprapubic catheter – the tube surgically inserted, a few inches below my naval, into my bladder to drain urine. My urethra had been severely torn and was beyond repair.

"Hmmm," she said, frowning, "I'll take a sample of that too." Erica collected the urine in a bottle. The urine looked dark and cloudy.

The suprapubic catheter increased the propensity for urinary tract infection, and the test results came back positive for a severe one. I had become a human Petri dish, home to a colony of mixed bacteria.

The catheter nurse arrived with a large green dressing pack. "Hello, my name is Rachael. I'm your urology nurse. We're going to remove your catheter and replace it with a newbie," she said, pointing at the suprapubic site. She tied on an apron and put on surgical gloves. "Let me see your wristband." She lifted my wrist, "Michael Tarulli, 10/05/1967 – that's you, yes?"

"Yep."

Tearing open the sealed pack, she lay the contents – including a long, brown, silicone-rubber catheter – on a sterile sheet. She lifted my gown, revealing my abdomen. "Michael," she said, drawing back the syringe, "I am removing water from the balloon that's holding the catheter." She shot a look at me; I stared back with nervousness. "Now relax." She tugged at the catheter. After a few attempts, the silicon tube failed to release. "I want you to breathe in and breathe out, ok?"

On the exhale, she pulled the catheter hard. The sensation was like yanking out my intestines. The catheter tip had crystallised with a build-up of calcium and magnesium phosphate, preventing its release from the bladder. My hands began to shiver.

"A little harder than I thought," she said, inspecting the stoma, the site of the inserted catheter. "Ok, we'll go again." She placed her fingers around the base.

I pushed her hand away.

"No!" she said, staring at me, reminding me of my grade six teacher. "Let's try this again together."

I tensed my abdominal muscles, hands gripping the bed sheets.

Rachael continued the disembowelment, twisting and tugging the catheter with force. The yanking finally gave way to a fountain of warm urine spilling over my abdomen. Rachel threw the old catheter aside and inserted the new one. She filled the balloon to hold the catheter in place. "All done," she said, smiling at last.

I cleared the tears from my eyes, thankful the ordeal was over.

The next time Dad came to visit I watched over him like a parent minding a child. He sat in his chair, playing with the drainage bag, picking up and dropping the tube to hasten the flow of the dark urine. I relaxed, not having to worry about him.

I was introduced to a chocolate-flavoured liquid diet via nasogastric intubation. A thin plastic tube was to run up the nose, down the throat, and into the gut to supply nutrients.

"Ready?" Erica said.

I sat up as far as my body allowed and closed my eyes as the tube went up my nose.

"Swallow the tube, Michael," she prompted.

I tried, gagging when the tube hit my epiglottis.

"Keep swallowing… swallow," she said, repeating like a parrot.

The tube got stuck. I tried. Tears flooded my eyes from the sensation. I reached out with blurred vision and grabbed her hand.

"Ok," she withdrew the tube "We'll try again in a few minutes. You ok?"

I slumped back into the pillow with sweat on my brow. "Yeah," I said with a croaky voice.

After two failed attempts, Erica sensed my growing frustration. On attempt number four, the tube made its way to the stomach. I could feel every inch of the worm-like conduit resting inside. I'd swallow saliva yet belch out acidic chocolate.

The grinding sound of the automated pump feed sounded like a growling dog, denying me sleep, night after night. I watched The Ashes to distract my mind, delighted to see David Boon scoring at will off the English bowlers.

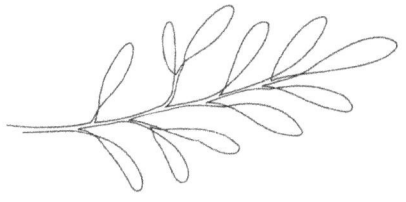

Big Jim

One night, as I lay on the bed, unable to sleep, I heard the helicopter's rotor blades chopping the air as it landed on the hospital roof. Minutes later the lights in our room were turned on with a flurry of voices. A new patient had arrived.

"Just inserting the needle, Jim," the nurse said. "There, this will help you through the night."

The sound of the infusion drip with its interval beeping started.

"You right now, Jim?" the nurse asked.

"Yes, all good… thank you." His accent suggested he was a Pacific Islander. He struggled, catching a breath between words. "Can you please, leave… the light on?"

"I'll leave the bed lamp light on for you, Jim."

"God bless… you."

The medical team left the room.

"Hello," the new guy called out.

The guy in bed one continued with his nasal chorus.

I turned my head towards the man they'd called Jim and noticed his head silhouetted by a halo. He looked solid, and large-chested. His bulging arms slumped over the bedsheets.

"Hello, can you... hear me?"

"Hi," I replied.

"Hello, my name is Jim. What's... your name?"

"Hi, Jim, my name is Michael."

"Ah, Michael... like Michael Jackson?"

"Yeah, like Michael Jackson," I laughed.

"Michael, I'm from... Nauru."

"You're a long way from home, Jim."

"Yeah, I came tonight... by plane." He took a deep breath. "Michael, I fell... off my motorbike."

I allowed the silence to swallow up his misery before opening up. "I had a car accident, Jim."

"Oh." He took a deep breath. "You married... Michael?"

"No."

"I am married... my wife, we have... six children."

"Ok." I paused and thought about what it would be like to be a father and a husband under the current circumstances.

"Do you believe... in God, Michael?"

I hesitated, careful with my answer. Though my heart was muddied with anger, and confusion was messing with my conscience, there was a belief. "Yes, I do, Jim."

"I believe in God... Michael. I will pray to God... for both of us." In the silence, he cried.

"I'll pray with you, Jim."

We developed a kindred friendship, sharing stories of sports and activities we had participated in our youth. He was familiar with "footy" (Australian rules), so we revived memories of famous players we admired and grand finals of the past. I can't remember who Big Jim supported. I nick-named him Big Jim owing to his solid frame. He spoke a lot about his home island Nauru, situated in the Pacific Ocean near the Solomon Islands.

"I'd like to come to Nauru and see you one day Big Jim."

"You are welcome... Michael."

It was Saturday night, and I was thinking about what Marcello and Chris might be doing.

My reverie was interrupted by Tom, the snorer from bed one. "Mike, do you want to watch this movie?" He held up a DVD. "I've watched it twice already. My wife hired it for me." Tom looked to be in his sixties, grey-haired and frail. "It's *Unforgiven*, with Clint Eastwood in it. Do you like Westerns?" His extended arm began to shake.

"Yeah, I don't mind a good Western." I sat up with the help of the overhang bar. "Haven't seen one for ages. I'll give it a go."

"This one's a ripper, you'll love it."

Veronica set up the DVD player and drew the curtain for my privacy. The movie triggered a tsunami of emotions. I gripped the bedsheets and picked at my fingernails, tearing them off millimetres at a time. I slammed my fist onto the mattress, yanking the nasogastric tube, which caused my eyes to water. The film was about a down-on-his-luck guy, Will Munny (Eastwood), who seeks revenge for the brutal death of his innocent friend Ned (Morgan Freeman) at the hands of Little Bill (Gene Hackman). The soundtrack at the end, with the lone tree shadowing, got to me; a tingling sensation spread across my face and the tears pooled in my eyes till they spilt over.

I lay awake thinking about the movie as Tom and Jim snored in synchrony. My mind drew comparisons with Will Munny: metaphorically, I, too, felt like I had been forced to my knees, been kicked in the guts, and crawled away in humiliation. The memories of being bullied at school, and the ill-treatment from those in the workplace solidified the internal pain and weakness I harboured for so long. The more I tried to ignore them, the harder the memories came to me.

I desperately tried to fit in at my training station at Caulfield Police back in 1990. One day I left my desk to take a tea break from the witness statement I was typing. When I returned minutes later, I noticed fellow officers Macca and Healey grinning slyly as they watched me take my seat. I found a large, enclosed envelope next to the typewriter with a sticky note penned "Constable Tarulli." I opened the envelope and pulled out a picture book titled *Officer Jim*. The first line greeted the reader, "This is Officer Jim…" It displayed a caricature of a smiling policeman. "Here, Officer Jim is helping school children cross the street…" I looked over at the pair, both broke out into hysterics. I dropped the book aside and shook my head.

I returned to typing, only to discover the detailed "I said/He said" statement had been tampered with. Someone had typed over the statement with foul language. I ripped the paper out of the platen and turned to face Macca and Healey.

"What's up, Mick?" Macca said, lifting the coffee mug to his lips.

I tried holding a brave front, "Real funny, guys." The humiliation was all too familiar, it reminded me of the bullying at school.

The pair continued laughing.

I scrunched the paperwork and threw it in the dustbin. I swivelled the chair back to begin my statement again. "Fuck'n idiots," I mumbled. The thought crossed my mind, *Maybe I'm not up to this*. I doubted my ability as a policeman, my confidence in the workplace was already low.

Kathy Armstrong, a visiting Sergeant from another station, witnessed the event. She approached me after they left and said, "Don't let the bastards get to ya."

But it was hard not to.

The humiliation of being labelled a "wog" in the 1980s returned to me. The brown-uniformed Ringwood Tech students would taunt me as I walked to school with my bag slung over my shoulder.

"Oi you, greasy WOG."

Hearing them yell that word was like a steel barb hooking into me like a targeted fish. I felt Mum and Dad's pain as if they were hearing the ugly word themselves. I understood my differences: I sported thick, dark hair, my skin was of olive complexion, I ate prosciutto and cheese sandwiches instead of the hundreds-and-thousands on buttered bread the other kids ate. I also inherited a "Roman nose" as Dad put it, much to my annoyance.

I'd stop, turn, drop my school bag, and rub my hands to loosen my fingers which had become rigid trapped between the handle and school blazer. I burned with rage.

"Whatcha gonna do, WOG?"

I'd grab my target by the collar and sleeve. Pulling him toward me, I'd throw him over my shoulder (called an *ippon* in judo). He would land on his back against the asphalt with a thud. I'd straddle his chest, striking his fleshy face with a clenched fist. "You were sayin'?" I said, striking him repeatedly. A crowd would gather, cheering me on. My rage was rooted too deep to stop. I repeated the blows, my right knuckles connecting with his lips and teeth, his face bloodied. "You give up? Had enough?"

My peers from Aquinas College took their turn, too. DJ, Manny and Ando would call out to me, "Ya WOG," or "Micky Twogy," The three were considered the "cool" guys in a mostly "white Aussie" school (there was one other second-generation Italian boy in my year level). As much as I was tempted to retaliate with fury, I feared that if I did so I'd become unpopular and alienate myself, so much so that I would break out into tears alone in the school chapel or toilet. Being a member of the school football team, and a competitive one at that, I had hoped would be a rite of passage to earn respect and be accepted as one of their own. However, the taunting continued. It was better to accept the verbal abuse and attain a pseudo-sense of belonging than to retaliate. In the later years of my schooling life, I obeyed the commandment of turning the other cheek: *Blessed are the peacemakers, doesn't it say in the Bible? For they will be children of God.* I thought all along that good would come from the refrain of fighting back. I was wrong.

I wrapped the overhang bar chain around my knuckles and made a fist. I stared into the dark space, breathing short and shallow as I stewed in silent anger. *I didn't fight back for the little guy; I let down young Michael.*

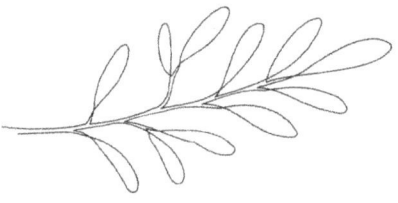

Blowfly

The days spent dormant in bed allowed me to reflect. Thoughts, like drops of water, soon became a flood of uncontrollable consciousness. *Was joining the Police Force to prove to my adversaries that I was worthy? A scream for attention? For my voice to be heard, rising above the roar of family and friends? Was it to combat feelings of resentment as the dutiful child? Or to reclaim the repressed youth, jilted by the lack of acceptance by DJ and company?* The gnashing teeth of regret bit hard into my memory cells. I thought of Caroline again. I imagined what it would've been like to be her boyfriend, to make love to her.

I asked myself if I had allowed Moyle to dictate terms on that fateful evening. *Did I allow him to silence my voice before the accident?* Like every missed opportunity, I imagined how life would've played out if I hadn't had the accident.

Every waking hour I was reminded of the past, of warning signs I should have paid attention to. I pulled the sheets over my bony body and head. Another memory brought on a shiver. *I should've taken Dad's advice early in my career.* I replayed the memory in my head. It was a Sunday at the tail end of 1990 and I had come to see the folks at the old home. I entered via the rear sliding door. "Hi, Mum."

"Michelangelo," she said in surprise, clasping her hands to her chest.

I reached my arms out and embraced her. She kissed me on the cheek.

"Hi, Dad," I said, looking over Mum's shoulder.

His blue eyes smiled. "Hello."

Both were in a good mood, and I was relieved.

"You want someting to eat?"

"No thanks, Mum. I ate already." I sat with my back to the wall, staring out into the backyard. Mum stood over the stove holding the tea towel as the coffee pot boiled. I loved the smell of fresh-brewed coffee. A sense of childhood comfort. A time when the world mattered not and the home was peaceful.

"You sure you no want coffee?"

"Nah, Mum."

"Where you come from?" Mum laughed. "You no like salsa or coffee."

"I'm a strange one, Mum."

"Tsk." She laughed.

The newspaper lay sprawled over the table. I brushed off the bread crumbs and picked up the sports page.

"How's work, Michal?"

I glanced over at Dad. "It's ok," I replied, shrugging my shoulders. I leaned forward, my elbows on my knees, turning the pages back to politics. Mum turned down the heat as the coffee pot made its spluttering sound, steaming at the spout. I could sense another question about to come at me.

"The bosses good to you? The people good to you?"

I stretched my neck from side to side. "Yeah, they're alright."

I leaned back on the wall and relaxed my shoulders, looking at the tall gum tree next door. Mum walked over and filled Dad's cup.

"Michelangelo, *una tazza di tè* (a cup of tea)?"

"No thanks, Mum."

"Why don't you work in the radio centre?"

"What? D24?" I said, looking up at Dad. To work in communications was seen by colleagues as a soft option, for those not wanting to do real police work. I noticed his eyes watering.

"I don't want you to get hurt, Michal," he said in a trembling voice.

"It's ok Dad," I said, trying my best to reassure him. "I can look after myself."

"Give the job away, if you don't like it."

His words were a punch of reality to the solar plexus. I was trying hard to guard my vulnerability.

"Nah, it's all good, Dad," I said, rubbing my nose with my forefinger and thumb. I dropped the paper onto the table and tapped my fingers on the laminated surface. I turned to him, "Don't worry, Dad – I'll be fine." I buried the doubt which gnawed away at my conscience, steeling myself to continue the charade, guarding my vulnerability.

I observed a fly buzzing in the corner of the screen. A blue-coloured blowfly was trying to free himself, beating his wings against the wire door. He bounced off the glass surface in a desperate attempt to find a way out. I became frustrated watching him go back and forth. *It's only inches to your left, you idiot. If you crawl to your left, you'll get out easily.* I knelt and carefully cupped my hand over the fly. I moved my hand toward the exit with the fly vibrating his wings against my skin. He found a gap and escaped my grasp. I tried sliding the flywire door to move him closer to freedom, without success. I sat down in frustration. "You can stay there."

The silence in the room became deafening. I picked up the newspaper. "What do you think of Jeff Kennett, Dad?"
   Dad shrugged his shoulders with a forlorn look.
   "Yeah, I think the same."

I dreamed I was in the dark, lying stagnant in my hospital bed. I became confused and lost, buried in excrement up to my neck. I could barely breathe, scooping aside the brown gooey mass in fear of drowning; my heart rate increased at the possibility. I pushed on, my arms breaking through, and arrived at a dark wooded forest; the air was clear and easier to breathe. Faint light penetrated the canopy to the forest floor as I crawled along. I reached the forest's edge at the mountain's peak, and there was Taka Sensei, greeting me with a smile. He outstretched his arm, pointing toward a double rainbow. The majestic colours in the sky lured me to the rainbow's origin. The years of absence between Taka and me didn't distort our friendship in this night story; our ties were as strong as ever.

I do wonder if the subconscious acts like a contingency model, willing the spirit to march on against adversity, or if one is conditioned to do so. I thought about this dream and its meaning for some time. Taka represented strength and hope, a timely reminder of the judo years when I was at my best. He showed me how to rediscover my ability to fight during fear and self-doubt.

Welfare

Veronica lifted the blinds, allowing the morning light to enter the room. I greeted my friend, the gum tree, with a smile.

"Good morning," Veronica greeted me.

"Morning," I replied.

"There are police officers here to see you." She waited for my reaction.

I gave her a blank look.

"They're from police welfare."

I sat up, "Ok."

Two officers arrived in plain clothes and introduced themselves. Leonie, who wore jeans and a polo top, and Alison, who wore formal trousers and a business shirt.

"How are you today, Mick?" Alison asked. "Can we call you Mick? Or do you prefer Michael?"

"Mick's fine," I said with a faint smile. I grabbed onto the overhanging bar to prop myself up. "I've seen better days."

"I bet," Alison said with a laugh. "We visited your Mum and Dad yesterday."

I fell into defence mode, not feeling comfortable hearing this. "How are they?"

"They're ok," Alison answered calmly.

I had a feeling she was holding back the truth. "You can be honest with me."

"They're coping ok, Mick." Alison moved her chair closer toward me. "We had a long chat with Mum, she's quite a character."

"Yeah, she is."

"She's close to you, yeah?"

I nodded. Mum remained steadfast and true. She wouldn't have held back with what she thought. I imagined her forthright vocabulary was used against the police hierarchy.

"Dad was a bit reserved, however."

"Yeah, that sounds like Dad."

"Don't worry; we're providing our full support for them." They both smiled to reassure me. "Is there anything you need?"

"Nah. I'm good for now."

Leonie moved in closer, brushing aside her hair. "Mick… Mark Moyle has asked to come and see you."

The sound of his name brought on fear and anger in waves. I dropped back onto the bed and stared at the ceiling, looking for the mouse smoking his pipe.

"How do you feel about him coming to see you?" Alison asked. "We can be present to support you if you like."

I turned to Alison. "No, I don't want to see him."

The pair looked at each other as I tapped at the overhang bar between the oscillating feelings. The silence between us thickened. I returned to the ceiling in search of the mouse.

Alison exhaled forcibly. "Have you thought about where you'd like to work when you get better?"

I shook my head. "No." I found and stared at the mouse with his pipe. I hoped the long pause would conclude our meeting.

"Ok." They both looked at each other. "We'll get going now, Mick," said Alison. "We'll come by again soon if you like us to?"

"Yeah, that'd be good," I said, forcing my smile.

I thought about the two women afterwards. They appeared genuine in their support. They also had a job to do; I understood that too.

My hair drooped over my eyes; bed hair became matted hair.

"I need a haircut. Is there a hairdresser in the house?" I asked the orderlies.

"You can book for the hairdresser," said Steve, with his hands beneath my torso, "but you might be waiting a while. They attend once a week and are usually booked out."

I placed my hands over my chest. The boys were in position.

"Ready?" Steve commanded. "On the count of three: one, two, three and lift." I was lifted and turned from my left to my right.

"I can give you a cut, Mike," Geoff replied, tucking the bedsheets under the mattress. "I've got an electric razor with clippers?"

Steve shook his head. "You trust Geoff to cut ya hair, Mike?" He looked at me with a half-cocked smile. "I've seen the result."

"He cuts like a sheep shearer," Andre said with a chuckle.

"Don't take notice of 'em," Geoff said, shaking his head, "I'll come back on your next turn with the electric razor."

"I dunno, Mike," Andre laughed.

Geoff arrived in the afternoon with the electric razor. "You want a number one, right?"

I nodded my head with unease. The clippers ran close to the skull, causing my head to vibrate, a liberating sensation. I watched the hair fall before my eyes. It reminded me of Dad in his barber days.

"Your hair is too long," Dad said. "You need a cut." As a child, Dad loved cutting my hair. He used his electric clippers, much to my displeasure. He wasn't a barber, though he liked to think he was.

"Come 'ere Michal," Dad called from the backyard. I peered out of the laundry window. He stood with clippers in hand, motioning me to come to the backyard. I shook my head.

He raised his voice, "Michal, now."

The beige kitchen chair was placed in front of him under the Hills Hoist. I dreaded losing my AC/DC style hair. He wanted me to look respectable and handsome.

"Michal, come 'ere now."

I stood at the kitchen door facing him. "I don't wanna short haircut, I wanna keep my hair long," was my protest song.

"Come 'ere and sit on de chair," he yelled with an angry bull-like stare. "De hair will grow back stronger; do you understand?"

It must have been true; I still have thick hair.

"America, America," Mum called out with one hand placed on her forehead, the other holding the laundry basket against her hip. This was what she said when trouble was brewing. I suspected it was Neapolitan slang.

I walked toward Dad at a snail's pace. Within reach, he gripped my arm and forced me down onto the chair. With clenched fists, I cried for him to stop; the buzzing sound of the clippers became angrier, the metal against my skull harsher. My thick, wavy, dark hair was removed millimetres from my scalp, from front to rear.

"Sit still, Michal."

I raised my eyes and noticed Marcello peering through the laundry window in tears; he was the next victim for the chair.

Back inside, I looked in the mirror and saw a haircut a drill Sergeant would be proud of. I pulled on the little hairs with my fingertips to increase their length before Monday's torment. "Please, hair, grow back," I said with tears rolling down my face.

"Hey, bald eagle," said the older kids at St John's primary, rubbing my head with force.

Mum and Dad arrived later that evening.

"Mamma Mia," Mum blurted. "What dey do to you?"

I laughed out loud. She held her hand over her mouth.

"Good haircut, Michal," Dad affirmed. To see him flicker a smile was a reprieve, the first in a long time. It brought me a sense of joy knowing there was a connection to the days of old, fresh-cut grass on football Saturdays and the smell of ripe tomato plants in the garden.

Mum took a wrapped figurine from her bag. She pulled apart the tissue paper and presented a statuette of the Virgin Mary, the same one I placed at the head of my bed at the Mitcham home. Mum wiped the laminated surface of my bedside drawer with a napkin. She placed Mary down. "Michelangelo, *la Madonna ti proteggerà* (Mary will protect you)."

I agreed to have her there, knowing it would please Mum. I felt embarrassed with Mary by my side, especially when people came to visit. I thought she'd give them the impression I was vulnerable, and therefore needed divine strength. Besides, my days of religious observance were no longer. To have her displayed next to me was meaningless.

Mum worked away, pressing on my legs like dough, her lips moving in silent prayer. Dad sat opposite her, lifting the catheter to speed the flow of urine into the bag. He stopped and took a device that resembled a belt sander with handles from a bag. "This will help you, Michal." Underneath the device were nodes designed to give deep tissue massage.

He plugged the electrical cord into a power socket and turned it on. "Is good for de circulation." He looked at me for my approval. He knew me too well – I was suspicious of the gimmick. He typically brought such gadgets, as seen in infomercials. He'd always comment on the product advertised and ask me, "Michal, get me one of dem, will you?"

"Dad, it's a sham, a waste of money."

He'd scrunch his face, disappointed with my judgement call.

I looked at the massager. "Dad, I don't want you to use that on me."

"Don't worry, dis will help you." He applied pressure as the device vibrated over my pelvis and legs, over bony joints and ligaments. My body jerked. There was only so much I could tolerate to please him.

"Dad, please, I don't like this."

"Just let me do it." His angry persistence was difficult to overcome.

"No." I matched his stare with my growing anger.

"Mick, enuff," Mum said.

Dad continued, concentrating on the areas close to the metal fixtures.

"Dad, please, it's not working for me." I reached out with my hands to convey my plea.

"Mick, *lascialo stare* (leave him be)," Mum said sternly.

Dad turned off the machine and looked up to the heavens with the look of the devil, teeth gritted and eyebrows pulled together with deep lines. "Fuck'n hell."

I wanted to fix his pain.

It was September, and time for the metal pins to be removed. Outside the operating theatre, I reached out to hold Veronica's hand.

"Will the pelvis hold up when they take out the pins?" I asked nervously.

"Well, you're not going to smash into a pole at high speed again, are you?"

I awoke from the anaesthesia, trying to fight off the grogginess. I looked at my torso; the Eiffel Tower was gone. My spirit lifted. Now I had the opportunity to be mobile again on a specially designed trolley bed, as I called it. This thing had a large wheel on either side, allowing me to balance and propel forward as I lay on my stomach. I ventured all around the hospital, exploring new grounds with enthusiasm. I smiled and waved at strangers – nurses, patients and cleaners – who all looked at me as though I was a sideshow.

The fun came at a cost. I lay in bed each night with aching muscles in my shoulders, back and neck. I'd move an inch of my shoulder or back, and the muscles screamed with pain. I took deep breaths before moving my body from side to side but the knotted muscles failed to uncoil. The pain was worth the freedom granted.

"Veronica?"

"Yes?"

"Veronica…"

She looked at me, frowning with curiosity.

"Veronica…" I said in a melodic tune.

"Oh, ok," she said, laughing. "It's not the first time I've had someone sing that to me."

"I want to use the trolley again."

She stood with folded arms. "Michael." She sounded like Mum. "Maybe give your body a rest?"

I looked at her, "Please?" I said with a smile.

I ventured far beyond my ward, rolling through the cardiac ward, the head trauma ward, and past the cafeteria. I continued down a vacant hallway to an abandoned space. I entered the old room, unsure of its use. The smell of a discarded banana peel overpowered the nasal senses. Sunlight filtered through the venetian blinds, catching the dust particles in the air. The room evoked a sense of tranquility, much like the chapel I visited at school. I looked up and noticed a glass cabinet that contained a black-and-white poster of Kate Moss, titled *Obsession*. I moved closer to inspect it. Her eyes were captivating, her lips shaped like rose petals, and her wet hair draped behind as though she had emerged from a lake in Arthurian times. I romanticised a fresh start, a renaissance of the heart and body with a desired woman such as her. I wanted to dream again, to believe I was worthy of attaining the unattainable. I felt at peace with this dream; it was just me and Kate and the lightness of being.

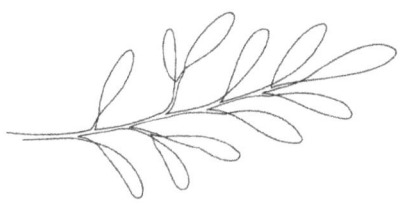

AIS

Anja walked up to my bedside after breakfast. "We empty the bowels now."

I cringed at failing to move my bowels on time yet again.

Anja inserted the suppository. "Ok, now we wait," she said, taking off her latex gloves. The colon bloated and squealed.

I shook with nervous tension. *Don't make this awkward for both of us, do your job.*

About fifteen minutes later, Anja returned. "How did we go?" She lifted the bedsheets and turned up my gown. I scrunched my eyes closed. Anja mumbled something in her native language. I had a bad feeling she was giving up on me, and so was my body.

The orderlies arrived about an hour later to change the soiled linen.

"G'day, Mike," Steve said. "How are ya?"

"Yeah, good." I lied.

Steve lifted the sheets, "Ah... change the sheets, boys."

I slapped the bed with an open hand. "Look, my body's forgotten how to work."

"Not your fault, Mike," Steve said, touching my shoulder for reassurance.

Anja arrived with a bucket of warm water and soap. I hated being cleaned up; the washcloth scrubbing against my scrotum and butt like I was an infant.

"Michael, sorry," Veronica said from behind the curtain. "There's a police officer who says you're expecting her?"

What luck I had with timing, I thought. *The smell of shit will hang around while we pretend it's not noticeable.*

"We won't be long," Anja replied.

I held onto the overhang grab bar and propped up on my elbow. My visitor walked in on time as agreed, wearing two stripes indicating her rank of Senior Constable.

For several months I had been avoiding the interview with the AIS. I refused their requests to interview me for some time. I was too afraid to relive the nightmare of the accident.

I finally agreed to be interviewed when police welfare contacted me about the investigators wanting to proceed. I knew well the time was right to do so.

"Hello Michael, my name is Kerry. I'm from the Accident Investigation Squad." She extended her hand to shake mine.

"Hi, Kerry." I liked her immediately; I sensed goodness about her.

Kerry sat down. "How are you today?" she said, holding the folder close to her chest.

I picked the skin off my index finger. "I'm ok, thanks."

"You didn't finish your meal?" she said, opening the folder with a pen at the ready.

I looked over at the half-eaten corned beef and cabbage sitting on the tray. "You call that a meal?"

She laughed. "Not the same as Mum's cooking, hey?"

"If you tasted my mum's homemade cooking, you'd agree."

"I bet… are you ready to begin?"

"Yes." I pressed my thumbnail into my palm.

"You understand why I am here?"

"Yes, to interview me about the car accident."

She nodded her head. "Ok, you ready to start?"

I nodded, running my hand over the prickly stubble of my haircut.

"Ok, Michael, tell me what happened from the beginning."

"I was the passenger in the police car, and Moyle was the driver. We received a 'shots fired' call from D24… when we were travelling along Lower Plenty Road at high speed with our lights on–"

"How fast were you travelling?"

"I'd say well over a hundred clicks."

"What happened next?" She looked at me with an expression of anticipated empathy.

I felt uneasy as I replayed the scene in my head. "A car entered the highway from the side street in front of us."

She lowered her eyes to the notepad, scribbling. "What happened then?"

"We steered in a direction to overtake the car in front. The same car tried to get out of our way but veered into our path."

"Can you describe that car to me?"

"It was a small car." I scratched my head, trying to remember the shape and colour. "I'm not sure what make it was."

She looked up. "You, ok?"

I nodded.

"Ok, what happened then?"

"We suddenly came up too close to the car in front. I froze. I remember stretching out my hand and pressing onto the dashboard." I pushed on, making the effort to say his name. "Moyle applied the brakes, and the car swerved. I remember sliding sideways toward the median strip."

"And then what happened?"

"I grabbed onto the Jesus bar above my head and braced for impact."

She looked at me, eyes widened, readying herself for the follow-up. "What happened next?"

"I hit the curb and felt intense pain on my left side. The second hit, I recall, was against the median strip guard rail, which was far worse." We locked eyes. "I wouldn't want my worst enemy to experience the pain I went through."

Kerry stopped, offering a sympathetic smile. "You ok to continue, or do you want a break?"

"Nah, it's ok."

She returned to her notepad. "Ok, what happened next?"

"I was stuck in the car and couldn't move; I was jammed in… I lost movement in my legs and started to panic. I found it difficult to breathe; at one stage, I thought I was gonna die." She continued scribbling away. If she was disturbed by my account, she didn't show it. I detailed the unfolding drama of extrication and being aided onto the gurney. The interview concluded.

Kerry placed the folder on her lap and sighed. "You ok?"

I nodded my head, "Yep."

"Never easy recounting the scene, is it?"

I shook my head, staring at the baboon's butt on the ceiling panel. "But ya gotta do your job, right?"

"Yep." She handed me the pen to sign the witness statement. "Please sign, below your name."

I was familiar with the process of signing my name next to the text that read "I solemnly and sincerely declare that the contents of this statement are true and correct and that this statement is signed with my true name and signature."

Kerry signed her name beneath as a witness. She smiled in acknowledgement. "Thank you for your cooperation, Michael."

I shook her hand and offered a tired smile.

"Well, have a speedy recovery," she said, holding the folder close to her chest.

"Thanks."

I was relieved the interview was finalised.

Shannon

Moving to rehabilitation meant I was getting closer to going home. The rehabilitation ward looked old, like a wooden dormitory that once catered for war veterans. The front door failed to close correctly, meaning a constant draft flowed through the corridor and into our rooms. I was introduced to using a wheelchair as my mode of transport; the ability to move from room to room, and even to the outdoor garden, was liberating. I felt more human than I had in months.

I shared a room with a fifteen-year-old named Shannon, who had a habit of making a clicking sound with his tongue. His mother and aunt came to visit daily. He had been hit by a car as he ran across the highway at night and had sustained a mid-torso spinal break.

"I reckon you're tall," he said. He was wearing his baseball cap backwards.

The truth is I was a short-arse. I figured my toned arms, and broad shoulders and chest gave the false perception of height.

"Nah, I'm not," I said.

I pushed hard on my wheels so that the front casters hung in the air. Shannon followed my action, adding a spin. I feared he'd turn away from me if he knew that I was a police officer, since he'd offered up his juvenile record to me. But he asked questions about my policing life that gave me a chance to gain his trust.

"Have you ever used your gun?" he asked with a cheeky grin.

"No. It's not like what you see in the movies."

He clicked his tongue. "Have you used the telephone book when beating someone?" he said, laughing.

"A few times."

His eyes widened as he dropped the front casters of his wheelchair to the floor.

"Just kidding." I chuckled. "I never did such a thing."

I had begun to feel as though my colon had a mind of its own. My stools moved willingly when I didn't want them to, and when they were expected to, they didn't. My assigned nurse for rehabilitation was Lyn, and we worked together on a bowel program to retrain my body to have regularity.

"He's a night man," Lyn called out. Shannon's mother, aunt and cousin were all within earshot outside our shared bathroom. *Oh great, tell the world.* I felt my face flush as I sat on the commode. My bowels moved at night as opposed to mornings, with the help of an enema.

"Finally," she said, throwing her hands up. "You're a regular in the evenings."

Lyn was a robust woman with fiery red hair, which matched her temper. Her nostrils flared when she was stressed or upset. I first witnessed this when I failed to notify her (or anyone for that matter) of my intention to leave the ward and explore the hospital surroundings. One night I sneaked out to see Big Jim in the spinal ward.

"Hello… Michael," Jim said, smiling and pleased to see me. He had the best smile. His neck brace prevented him from turning his head, so he followed my movement with his eyes.

"Hi, Big Jim."

His once-bulging arms were thin as matchsticks, lying motionless on the bedsheets, and his pectoral muscles had diminished. I watched his chest rise and fall with shallow breaths.

"You still pray… Michael?"

I wheeled up to Jim and held his hand. "Yes, Jim. I pray for us both."

I didn't. I used these words to keep his spirits up.

On my return to the rehabilitation centre, Lyn stood at the door, waiting for me with folded arms and flared nostrils, shaking her head. "And where have you been? We were looking for you everywhere."

I couldn't help but regress to the days at Aquinas College when I was chastised by the teacher for being late for class because I had I overstayed my time in the chapel.

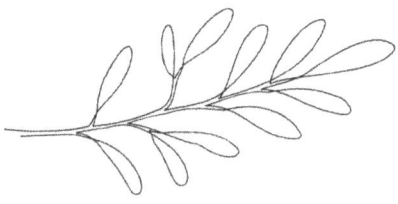

Night Shift

My cousin, Bina, came to visit me, accompanied by her German boyfriend, Uwe (pronounced *oo-vuh*). I hadn't seen her since she left for London in the late 80s, before I joined the police. I felt like I was masquerading in her presence, pretending everything was ok. In our youth, we had talked about travel and dreams. She knew of my sentimental nature; she knew the uniqueness of my being. I felt awkward in her presence.

Bina's surprise visit reminded me of something I had been contemplating before the accident, and a conversation I had had with Wayne Keough about taking leave from the police.

Whenever I entered Heidelberg Police Station to commence work I felt a sense of anxiety. I was relatively new and felt I was being judged by the sergeants and veteran senior constables. I preferred the night shift; policing was made bearable with fewer people around. Bringing in Mum's homemade lasagna and gnocchi to share earned a degree of popularity with other members. I shared van duty with Wayne on night shifts, and he was always one to lend an ear. He had a calm demeanour that made me feel at ease, and I felt confident working in his company.

One night in February 1993, the heat and humidity had driven us to get raspberry Slurpees from a 7-Eleven store. Back in the car, the radio fell silent and I confided to Wayne about my on-and-off relationship with Leah.

"What seems to be the problem?" he said, driving along the highway.

I stared through the passenger side window. "I dunno," I replied. But I did know.

"Hmm, have you spoken to her about how you feel?"

"Kinda." I dropped the pen on the notepad and folded my arms. "We end up arguing all the time."

"Do you love her?"

I turned to Wayne, surprised at the direct question; it was uncommon to talk about one's feelings at work, particularly among male colleagues. I took a deep breath as we stopped at the red traffic light. "I can't seem to move on from her."

"Why do you say that?"

"Coz… I dunno."

"Must be a reason."

I squirmed on the passenger's seat, tapping the pen against the notepad.

Wayne turned side-on, waiting for my answer. "What is it?" he asked.

"I feel like she's got a hold on me… and… I can't let go." I let out a deep sigh, wanting to move on from the subject. "I'm considering applying for leave without pay."

"You what?"

"Yeah, I want to go overseas. Start in London, then travel

around Europe." The traffic light signal changed to green. I watched the streetlights flash by, searching for answers in the dark. I thought of Caroline, picturing her smile and piercing blue eyes. I harboured guilt for thinking of her, longing for her. The last I heard she was living in London. The thought of being close to her, sharing the same city, was enough to excite my senses. I imagined bumping into her. Or, she may get word that I was in town and search me out. The thought that she may have a boyfriend, or be married, didn't cross my mind.

I felt alive again in my cousin's presence, daring to dream. London was calling. I had the feeling it was calling me.

Girls

The bedroom window was open every day, allowing the fragrance of spring acacias to flow in during the afternoon, much to my satisfaction.

One day, as Shannon wheeled his chair back and forth in the one spot next to his bed, he opened up. "Hey Mike, do you think you'll walk again?"

I dropped the front casters of the wheelchair onto the rickety floorboard. "I don't know, mate," I said with an exasperated breath. I looked away toward the open window. The trees outside reminded me of the secret pact I made with my friend, the gum tree.

"They say in ten years," he paused, "in ten years, there'll be a cure for us paras."

I turned to meet him at eye level. "We can always have hope, yeah?"

"Yeah." He clicked his tongue. "Hey, can you get a hard-on?" he said jokingly.

"No."

"Yeah, same," he said with head bowed, picking at the cushion of his wheelchair. "What do ya reckon," he said with a serious tone. "Would girls still dig ya if ya can't get it up?"

"I think girls dig you for who you are, not if you can get it up," I answered. I had given it much thought, and I, too, struggled with this question and the simpleness of my answer. The spectre of doubt crept in as I lay in bed wondering if women would consider me, an impotent man in a wheelchair, desirable.

Long into the dark night, I heard his muffled sobs. The room's stillness thickened; you could almost feel its sad texture. My heart sank for the boy.

"It's all right to cry, mate. I cry too, sometimes."

Kev

I was sitting in the courtyard one afternoon, watching the wattle birds frolic in the garden, when a dishevelled man in his thirties crashed his wheelchair through the exit door.

"G'day, me name's Kev," he said as he approached me.

"Hi. I'm Michael."

"I've heard about you… so you're a cop?" He said in a rowdy manner.

My nerves fired off. "Yeah, that's right." I anticipated a hostile reaction.

He leant in close. "I got shanked in the slot," he said with excitement. "The bloke came up from behind, didn't see it comin." He took off his singlet to show me the scar.

Could this get any weirder? Me and a prisoner under the same roof.

"The bloke jammed a makeshift knife in me back," he said, demonstrating a thrusting action with his hand.

I watched on like a spectator observing a theatre performance.

He lifted his legs, said, "I can't move em," and let them drop. "See, I'm fucked." He lit up his cigarette. "What happened to you?" He waved the matchstick to put out the flame.

I suspected he knew already, but he wanted to hear the story from me. "I had a car accident."

He blew out a steady stream of smoke. "Shit mate, how did it happen?"

I rubbed my chin, "I was on police duty. We responded to a 'shots fired' call. A car from the side street ventured into our path, and the rest is history." I didn't want to go into details with him.

"Shit… Fucked, hey?" He flicked his cigarette to get rid of the ash, "See? We're no different, mate, you and me." He folded his tattooed arms. "We're both paras, both fucked."

Think of England

Kathleen was my physiotherapist for the duration of my rehab. "Ok, let's go for a swim," she said in her posh English accent. The hydraulic device held me with its sling, lifting and cradling me like a baby, transporting me from the wheelchair and into the pool. I reached out to Kathleen, waist-deep in water.

"And here we are," she said, wrapping her arms around my torso. Her slender body rubbed against my feeble frame. I'd forgotten how soft and inviting it felt to caress a woman's body. She then let go of me, like a fairy dandelion into the breeze of the water. I moved my arms and legs, like a paddling dog.

"You okay?"

"Yeah," I said with caution. The transparent liquid was a moving body, enveloping my bony frame and odd-shaped pelvis. I squirmed inside from the bizarre feeling of this. No longer were my arse muscles sculpted from swimming or running. My legs were dead weight, like broken branches from a tree trunk. The cold claimed whatever warmth was left in me. I surrendered to it. Water crept up into the crack of my arse and invaded my rectum. *That's a first* (I had lost control of the sphincter muscle). It didn't take long for the nerves in the butt hole to be aggravated. I tried to ignore its sharpness and continued with my weightless dog paddle exercise. I must've looked helpless.

"It's ok, I got you," Kathleen said, dragging my wilted body in close. She turned me around, my eyes facing the ceiling, my heartbeat racing. "Relax now." She held me under the armpits, "And here we go." With her guided hand, I floated on my back, my head nestled in her cleavage; the shape of water flowing over my chest, throat and face. "Just relax and think of England."

Why would I want to think of England?

Her grip brought back memories of Mentone Beach in the summer with the family. Dad held me tight as my tiny limbs climbed onto his shoulders to dive off and into the waters of Port Phillip Bay.

I looked forward to the next physio session, resting my head against Kathleen, thinking of England.

Taka

My old friend, Ged, surprised me with an impromptu visit. My heart leapt at his familiar smile, which hadn't changed since our school days. We had been school buddies and fellow competitors in school cross country and athletics. He left our shores for Japan not long after he gained his teaching degree at university. He taught English at an international school in Tokyo. It must've been in the late 80s when I last saw him. His tall, lean frame would've been quite the novelty in Japan, particularly his curly red hair. He had heard about my accident on his arrival back in Australia.

Standing next to him was a young lady.

"Mick, this is my wife, Aiko," Ged said.

"Hello," she said in a soft voice, bowing her head with a sorrowful expression on her face. She reminded me of Taka's wife, Hideko. I replied in kind.

"How are ya, mate," Ged said, rubbing my shoulder.

I felt my cheeks blush. "I'm doing ok."

He tried hard to hide his sadness with his smile, looking down at the sight of my emaciated body. I needn't have told him of my physical prognosis; he knew. I changed gears to disrupt the discomfort.

"So, mate, how's life in Japan?"

Ged spoke of Tokyo life and his teaching job.

As he did so, I felt the emotional attachments to Taka; judo and Japan began to re-awaken. I remembered the days of the dojo, Taka walking on the judo mat like a Buddhist monk. With arms behind his back, he'd call out the instructions, "Ichi… ni… san." A tall man, his dark brown complexion, high cheekbones and square jaw made him handsome. He possessed nobility and calmness, both of which I admired.

"Like this, you see, he can't get free," he'd say with a steely look in his eye, demonstrating a stranglehold. "Good… good," he said, placing a hand on my shoulder. We knelt in a row on the judo mat. He nodded, instructing me to take the class through meditation.

"Breathe in… breathe out. Breathe in… and out," I called to the class.

I also had the pleasure of meeting the Takatera family at dinner. Dad dropped me off in Clayton at Taka's house, a cream-coloured brick building with wattles in the front yard.

"Please come in," Hideko said, smiling.

"Thank you," I said, bowing to her with clumsiness. I took off my shoes before entering. Stepping inside, the home was another world. There was a bonsai plant in the hallway, wooden floors and paper walls. I followed Hideko to the dining room, where I sat at a low table; there were no chairs, and we sat on the floor, cross-legged. Hideko apportioned small bowls of food with graceful hands. Their little boy, about six, and his younger sister watched me take on sashimi laden with wasabi. When the heat erupted in my sinuses, the children burst out laughing as I squeezed out the tears. Taka rebuked them in Japanese. I composed myself and smiled at them.

In 1984, Taka and Hideko decided to return to Japan. The news hit me hard. I'd known Taka since I was eight years old. He was my hero. A testimonial was held at Mitcham High School in honour of his services to Judo Australia. At the close of the ceremony, Mum and Dad presented a parting gift. Taka unwrapped the parcel and held up a bronze miniature replica of the Leaning Tower of Pisa. He inspected the ornament, "Oh, very nice." I doubted he knew what it was.

"It's the Leaning Tower of Pisa, a famous building in Italy," I said.

"Thank you," he said, bowing his head. He handed the gift over to Hideko, who held it out in front of her, smiling and nodding as a thank-you gesture.

My concealed tears swelled as I looked Taka in the eye, shaking his hand for our final farewell. He smiled and placed a hand on my shoulder, no words spoken. He departed with his family, turned around one last time and waved goodbye. I followed Mum and Dad out of the hall and into the cold night. I felt hollow, like a part of me had been separated. I wondered whether I'd see him again.

After Ged and Aiko left, I sat on my bed, alone, thinking of the past. I wanted to relive the passion that burned so bright during my judo years. There, in my heart, was a desire to visit Japan and seek out Taka. I needed to see him in the hope he could repair my damaged soul.

Floppy Eggplant

I was introduced to a young occupational therapist who showed me the layout of a mock dwelling with accessible features; from the kitchen bench to the workbench, all were waist-high and clear for the wheelchair to fit under.

"Make yourself at home," she said.

I rolled up my sleeves and donned an apron to make sausage rolls, wrapping big, meaty pieces in puff pastry. I offered them to my family on their visit; Marcello helped himself to a second serving. *Good to know his appetite hasn't changed.*

I constructed a large wooden chopping board for Mum and Dad to cut meat and slice crusty bread. The activity lifted my energy, reminding me of woodwork at school.

My memories went back to other items I had made: the fish-shaped trivet that protected the tabletop from the pasta-sauce pot and spaghetti bowl; the timber bar stool with rattan cushion that Mum used for drying clothes in front of the gas heater; a step ladder that Dad used to hang homemade salami in the cellar adjoining the garage.

The one thing I always wanted to discuss – with whoever cared to listen – was the matter of sex after spinal cord injury. I felt the subject was almost taboo to raise with Lyn. I was too worried that she'd flare her nostrils and shake her head, admonishing me like a school teacher. I summoned the courage to ask her on one of her morning rounds. "Lyn… I want to know about options with… you know, sex."

She raised her eyebrows and flared her nostrils. "I'll get you to watch a video; it will explain all you need to know and everything to do with that, ok?"

I nodded in agreement.

Lyn placed the VHS tape into the video player and pressed play, "I'll leave you to it." She walked out of the TV room, closing the door behind her. The video revealed what I already knew: I couldn't have a normal erection due to the damage to my lumbar and sacral areas.

My frustration began to build; I bit down on my fingernails to the point of reaching the reddish skin. The weeks were counting down before I was to be discharged for home life. I had heard of synthetic methods to sustain an erection from other patients in the ward. I summoned my courage weeks later when a young doctor, who looked to be an intern, approached and greeted me on her morning rounds.

"Um… can I ask you a question, please?" I flicked my eyes over to Lyn, who stood with pursed lips and a *what are you going to say?* look.

"Yes," the doctor replied.

I started to pick the skin around my index finger. "I wanna know… if I can get an erection again? Like… is there anything I can use to help get one?"

"There are several options available to you," she said confidently, raising her eyebrows. "A specialist nurse in urology can offer you alternatives to achieve a sustainable erection."

I glanced over to Lyn; her face matched the colour of her hair. The young doctor turned to Lyn, instructing her to organise a consultant to meet with me. Lyn nodded, stabbing the pen onto the notepad.

"The nurse will organise that for you." She smiled cheerily at me. "Is there anything else, Michael?"

"No, thank you, doctor."

A week later a young woman in her forties arrived holding a large plastic bag. "Sorry I'm late," she said, greeting me warmly. "I'm the urologist nurse. Michael, is it?"

I noticed her chewing gum. "Yes," I replied.

She laid out the contents from her bag onto my bed. There were devices I assumed were to enhance penile erection. *Christmas has come early.*

"I'll explain these to you in a minute," she said, looking me straight in the eye with empathy. Her breath smelled of stale cigarettes.

"Are you in a relationship Michael?"

"No."

She scratched her upper lip. "That's ok."

Why do I get the impression her hesitation is not a good sign.

"I'm going to show you these mechanical aids and how they work." She picked up what looked like a plastic bong. "Now, this is a pump called Vacuret…" She went through the steps of its function, explaining that the Vacuret was designed to inflate the phallus by drawing veinous blood to the penis body. The second option was a solution called Caverject that was injected into the penis body; the needle had to be inserted at the precise location for it to take effect. The third option was a penile implant.

"This, I highly recommend," she said. "I've heard nothing but good feedback about the penile implant from clients."

I felt squeamish on hearing this. "How do the implants work, like… what's involved?"

"The muscles that facilitate the erection are surgically removed." She showed me a diagram. "These inflatable cylinders replace those muscles. A valve is placed in the penis along with a fluid pump in the scrotum. This is used to inflate the implants, mimicking an erection."

I felt like she was trying a Tupperware hard sell.

"It's ok. You have time to try the first two options and think about the last one, ok?"

What other options do I have? "Ok."

I lay on my side, alone in my room with the door closed. The bed hardened as I curled up my knees, pondering a life of impotence. A part of my youthful spirit was taken away, like I was robbed. The tears were silent. I reflected on my time at the university library, reading up on this for my nursing degree. Anger and disbelief flowed in and out like ocean tides.

I tried the Vacuret on myself. With the rubber ring on the base of my penis to restrict the venous blood from escaping, I pumped away at it like a bike pump. To my disappointment, the result was a purple erection, much like a floppy eggplant. I turned to the Caverject; the stiffened phallus took on the shape of a cigar, with a distinctive bulge in the middle. I was disheartened by the result of this too. *No penis deserves to experience such brutality.*

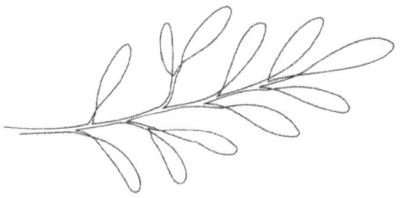

Do I belong here?

It was a matter of days before my discharge when Mark O'Connor, a colleague from Heidelberg Police, surprised me with a visit. He was the last of my colleagues I thought would make the effort to see me. Mum and Dad sat beside me as I rested on the bed, wearing my Nike tracksuit. O'Connor, in uniform, was accompanied by a young male constable who I didn't recognise.

O'Connor greeted me casually. "How are you feeling?"

"I'm not too bad."

"I hear you're going to be discharged soon, yeah?"

"Yep. It's the food – it's terrible."

He chuckled, "That's good, mate. Nothing beats Mum's homemade cooking, hey?"

"Mum, Dad, this is Mark."

He turned to Mum and Dad. "Hello, Mr and Mrs Tarulli," he said, removing his police hat. "My name is Mark O'Connor. I work with Michael."

"Hello," Dad said hesitantly. Mum nodded her head, barely moving her lips in greeting him. I sensed their unease; it was like two worlds colliding. Their facial expressions were a giveaway, both stared at our unannounced visitor, their thoughts weaving between curiosity and suspicion, unsure whether our guest was friend or foe (the driver on the fateful night of the crash).

O'Connor was a paradoxical individual. I couldn't work him out.

My memory took me back to early 1993 when I was relatively new at Heidelberg Police Station. I was the watch-house keeper that evening when a young woman came in and walked towards the counter. She appeared agitated, gasping for air; her white sports jacket had bloodstains on the front. She looked no more than twenty-five, her pretty face defined by years of hardship. I noticed her left eye bulged bright red.

"I like to report my boyfriend; he went crazy on me, the motherfucker."

"You, ok? Do you need to go to the hospital?" I asked.

"Nah, I'm right, just mad as fuck."

"Ok, just calm down. I'll need to take a statement from you." I took a photo of her battered eye.

"He hit me on the head, too," she said, touching the impact area.

I separated the hair strands and noticed an abrasion. "I will need a medical report of your injuries. You will see a doctor, yes?"

"Yeah, if you say so."

I held my pen over the report. "Your name?"

"Amanda… you can call me Mandy," she said, clearing her hair away from her face.

"Surname?"

She paused. "Dennison."

"Ok, Mandy, can you tell me what happened from the start?"

I heard laughter from the rear section of the station as the van crew arrived with their dinner. O'Connor walked past the interview room and the smell of fish and chips wafted in. He stepped back and peered through the door; I felt his judgement burning into my conscience. I was always on edge in O'Connor's presence. He'd look at me so intensely that I could almost peel his eyes off me with a spatula, and he never smiled. He had a habit of clicking his pen with his thumb, clicking on-click off, clicking on-click off.

"What are you staring at?" Amanda yelled at him.

I wanted to bury my head.

"You don't ask questions; we do," O'Connor replied with fire.

"There's one good copper in this joint, at least."

"Can I see you for a minute?" O'Connor indicated for me to follow him.

"Wait here, Mandy; I'll be back in a minute." I walked out of the room and met with O'Connor.

"Mate. Do you know who she is?" He said, pointing with his thumb.

I shook my head, waiting for an answer.

"She's a Dennison. The whole family is feral. Her old man is serving time, and her brothers are scrotes."

I felt my face flush, and my heart raced with humiliation.

His eyes remained fixed. "Mate, get rid of her."

Thoughts flooded through me in the milliseconds that followed. *Do I belong here? Am I competent at my job?* The fear of judgement was raw; I knew I couldn't let slip any sign of sensitivity or weakness. But anger brewed inside me. "She's come to report an assault. I'm just doin' my job." I walked off with heavy feet and resumed the interview. I heard a chuckle from the corridor. I sat down in front of Mandy, who remained with folded arms and a stern look. "Ok." I let out a deep breath, "Continue from 'He pushed me against the wall.'"

The doubt inside me continued to nibble away but I refused to acknowledge its presence, I preferred to continue masquerading in my blue uniform.

O'Connor had always seemed aggressive and unfriendly, yet here he stood, hat clutched to his chest, speaking to me as if these were my last days on earth.

"Ok, we won't take up your time," he said, smoothing out his hat.

Mum, Dad and I watched as he donned his hat, with his colleague doing the same.

"Take care, buddy."

"Thanks, mate," I replied. I watched him walk out with his companion following behind. I felt O'Connor wanted to bridge the divide that separated us. And that beneath the surface he wasn't such a bad guy.

"Who was dat person, Michal?" Dad asked with a frown.

I looked over at Mum. I could tell she was eager to know too. They were asking whether O'Connor was the driver.

"That was Mark." I raised my hand to reassure him. "Don't worry. He's ok."

"What is his surname?" asked Dad, leaning with his ear in my direction.

"O'Connor."

"What did he want?"

"He just came to visit."

Dad leaned back on his chair, clasped his hands, and resumed his Buddha-like pose. Mum proceeded to massage my legs in an attempt to heal them, as she always did.

Home Again

In November 1993 I returned home as a stranger. The air inside the house I shared with Mirella was filled with the scent of the roses that grew beneath the open windows; the same roses I pruned and pricked my fingers while gardening. The Baltic pine floorboards creaked as I wheeled between rooms. I ventured into my bedroom, the cover of my doona was washed and ironed, and the white sheets were tucked neatly under the mattress – Mum had prepared the bed for my homecoming.

I pulled out a box of sporting paraphernalia hidden in the corner of the room. It contained my track shoes, flattened from the weight of a dumbbell, a pair of football boots with their leathery odour, and the Mustangs football jumper with the yellow number forty on the back. Intense feelings of youthful energy flowed through me. I lifted the prize of the lot: my judo bag, given to me by Taka. The white satchel consisted of heavy woven fabric; the black Japanese inscription on its face had faded. I stuck my nose in and smelled memories of competition and glory days. I wondered about Taka and what became of him. The culmination of these sporting memories flashed like a film projector; images of my able body going into action.

I rolled into the shared walk-in wardrobe that stood between Mirella's and my bedroom. I opened some drawers and noticed socks, shirts, underwear and trousers I didn't recognise. Realising these items belonged to Mirella's boyfriend, Gareth, my temper reached boiling point. I slammed the drawers back and punched the wall, "FUCK!" The invasion of my space felt like denial of my existence. The thought that I had been reduced to a lesser being, to the point of insignificance, became tangible.

I moved to find comfort in the lounge room. The space there was always calming for me. Staring at the ferns kept me suspended, like I was in a trance, beyond the French windows. The plants that made up the garden appeared calm and at peace; the sun's light providing them with energy to grow and bloom. Their presence distracted me from the reality of my disability, sitting on a padded cushion on a chair with wheels.

I turned to the wooden coffee table that my young hands had cut and shaped at Aquinas College. I bent down to feel its earthy grain, its chiselled legs and routed edges. I ran my hand over the smooth finish as sunlight shone against the surface. *It's like I worked on this beauty yesterday.*

Then the silence hit me. An overwhelming fear gripped my heart; a black hole opened like a chasm. Tears broke free, running down my cheeks. I looked up and yelled out to the God I thought I knew. "Why? Why did you do this to me?" I begged hard for answers, "Why me?" The tears obscured my vision as hurt spilt over the tear ducts. The weight of my body could no longer hold up; sorrow sapped my strength. I slumped to the floor, crying with gasps for air, my knees pressed against my chest. The emptiness swallowed what self-worth I had left. I crawled on my elbows and lifted the telephone off the receiver. I dialled the number. "Mirella… I need you to come here… PLEASE."

I waited. Thoughts lingered on like a melody. No longer was I being fed, washed and mothered. The truth hit me hard. Never had I imagined this could happen; I feared what lay ahead. The smell of dust and the taste of tears brought on the burning questions: *Am I imagining all this is truly happening to me?* I swallowed hard and returned to the feeling of my bony hips pressed against the floor; the empty wheelchair watched over me. I listened to the sound of my rhythmic heartbeat till I closed my eyes and fell asleep.

Mirella arrived first, followed shortly after by the spinal outpatient nurse, Chloe, who had been assigned to visit me weekly after my discharge. Chloe held my hand as I lay on the bed. "Michael, it's OK to feel this way." She dipped her head to look me in the eye, "You're home again… it will take time to adjust."

I nodded my head for the sake of agreeing with her.

I hated the foreigner living in my bladder, the indwelling catheter. It tugged at my insides when I turned in my sleep. The pain in my hips magnified when my body rested. I lifted the doona and mapped the contour of my body. I felt the outward shape of my pelvis. The left side was still lower than the right. "FUCK!" I shouted.

Mirella opened the door, switching my bedroom light on. "Michael?"

"My hips are out of shape," I yelled. "And this," I showed her the catheter, "This is pissing me off."

"Michael." She brought her hand to her chest. "You just have to get used to it."

Angry tears flowed down my cheeks.

"Michael?" she whimpered.

"And what happened here?" I said, running my hand over my left torso, "I don't have muscle there." I slammed my fist onto the mattress.

"Michael, they saved your life. They did everything possible to save you."

I punched the wall beside me, leaving a hole in the plasterboard.

"Please stop!"

I placed both hands on my head, still fighting off the reality of what had occurred seven months ago, refusing to digest the truth.

"Please, get some sleep, Michael."

I couldn't sleep; the darkness consumed me.

The house of three was too crowded. Gareth was a temporary live-in, strangling my space, and my resentment towards him was starting to show. Not only did Gareth take over my chest of drawers with his leopard print underwear and khaki socks, he spoiled my fridge with leftovers from his home-cooked meals, reeking of garlic; my boronias had been neglected and left to die, replaced by alien plants of his choosing. And most frustrating, Gareth held the TV remote.

I expressed my desire to be alone, and so my wish was granted. Mirella and Gareth agreed to move out and bought a house of their own in Richmond. I relished the solitude; to finally breathe easy was a God-send. I reclaimed my castle and playground; I was in control of the remote, and – with extendable tools to work with – the rebirth of my garden was under way.

Nights alone provided me time to read my forgotten favourites, Che Guevara and Malcolm X. I heard their voices lift from the pages, language resonating with my rage and personal revolution. I recalled writing an essay on Martin Luther King Jr. in my humanities course at Box Hill TAFE, in 1987, noting his mantra on nonviolence in the pursuit of redemption during the Civil Rights movement. Boundaries and obedience were all I knew in my youth. But my days as a peacemaker amounted to an empty fortune. I wrestled with Catholic indoctrination to the point of blaming the ideology for all my misfortune. My thinking was that I had been sucked in at an early age and my freedom and independence had been taken away from me. I picked up the diamond tumbler and took another swig of scotch. I turned on the stereo and played the pulsating beats of AC/DC to match my temper. I refilled the glass and raised my hand in salute, "To you, Malcolm X, you were right all along."

I opened the back door and rolled out onto the wooden patio facing the backyard. The cool air and screeching bats made for a lovely evening. With legs crossed, I lit up my first cigarette, drew in the first breath and exhaled a steady stream of smoke. I started smoking in defiance of life, disregarding my health. I smoked to revive the memory of Nonno Joe, wearing his fedora, sitting cross-legged while sipping cappuccino. The lightness of my head made for fond memories. I amused myself with the memory of his customary hand gestures: he'd tug his bottom eyelid with his index finger, indicating "pay attention". He'd also press his forefinger against his thumb, and move his hand horizontally away from his mouth, like plucking a guitar string – this gesture meant one was smart or clever.

The resident possum in the gum tree made a grunting sound.

"What's ya problem?" I called out.

I looked up at the vast stars, shining like diamond pebbles. The Southern Cross was easily found, and the Saucepan too. I located a cluster of stars, and stared at them. I spoke to the stars as though they were long-lost friends. *The distance between us is far, yet your brilliance is within reach. If only I could embrace you.* They remembered me from earlier days when I had lain down with my back on the grass, telling them of my love for a girl at school.

Bad Moon Rising

About two months after Mirella left home, I began drinking at liberty – regularly and alone. The frail image of my body in the mirror, sitting in the wheelchair, and the loss of my sexuality ate away at my conscience. I drank beer and spirits nightly to numb my head.

Picking up the cardboard box and tipping out its contents, I chose Rage Against The Machine for the evening. With whiskey in hand, I romanticised my self-imposed prison. I rediscovered Iggy Pop after years of absence. I moved to the melancholic tunes of Queen and Talking Heads. The cover of The Reels's *Requiem* caught my eye, a stark reminder of the night before my accident. I remembered it well – it was the last night of my days off, my freedom too short before my fateful shift with Moyle. Mirella and Gareth headed out for the evening; and I welcomed the opportunity to be alone. I recall sitting on the pine floorboard with my back to the wall, meditating. The loungeroom was alight with candles. The effect cast shadows on the walls; the shapes moved like ghosts, producing an eerie feeling. I stood up and walked over to the oval-shaped mirror above the mantlepiece. I stared at myself; my expression was one of melancholy, my relationship with Leah had come to an end, but the emotional ties remained. I massaged my head with both hands, asking my brain for forgiveness. I resumed my seated position with my back against the wall, thinking about the waitress I had begun dating at Denny's restaurant. I needed to move on from Leah and the lingering thought of Caroline.

The haunting sound of "Bad Moon Rising" commenced on the stereo. I stared at the candle on the mantelpiece, hypnotised by its mirror image. The blurring colours of yellow and orange swirled with intensity. I went with its magical flow and became aware of another's presence. The shadow on the wall grew larger and darker. I curled up with my legs tucked in. I thought my mind was playing tricks.

I continued listening with the stranger by my side, fighting off the discomfort yet accepting him in the empty silence.

The strange experience with my phantom friend stayed with me the next day, 16 April 1993. Restless thoughts and discomfort stuck with the feeling of staleness. I walked into the watch house to sign in for my firearm.

"I'm driving," Mark Moyle called out, showing me the car keys. I acknowledged Moyle with a nod of the head. My feet weighed heavy as I walked along the corridor, like moving through a morass. I sat down in the mess room and rubbed the back of my neck as Sergeant Driscoll commenced his briefing.

"Keep a lookout for a male suspect fitting this description," he held an identikit aloft. "He's known to loiter around the Bell Street Mall dealing…"

I stared at the corners of his mouth; one side bore a red swelling, dipping lower than the other as he spoke.

"Ok, any questions?" No one answered. "Good. Go about your duties."

I stood up and walked out of the cluttered room, avoiding eye contact with my peers. The toilet was a temporary refuge, the air easier to breathe while taking a piss. I returned to sorting the relevant forms and equipment for the Falcon sedan, our patrol car. Meanwhile, Moyle leaned against the file cabinet, swinging the car keys around his fingers. He looked over and noticed me staring, "We good to go?"

I picked up the patrol kit and turned toward the exit door. "Yep, ready when you are."

"Heidelberg 206 Code 1," I radioed to D24.

"Roger Heidelberg 206."

Moyle looked at himself in the rear-view mirror, brushing his hair back. The sense of superiority radiated off him as I sat in the passenger's seat, taking notes.

About an hour into the shift, the radio crackled. "Shots fired," the operator announced.

Moyle planted his foot on the accelerator.

I returned to the tumbler of whiskey and swallowed what remained of the amber liquid. As the night grew old, I desired a woman's body. She was only a phone call away.

"Your lady's name is Sheree. She will arrive at your front door in half an hour," the female voice at the end of the line said.

It wasn't the first or the last time. She'd face me, straddling me with her legs on either side of the wheelchair; my hands would move gently over her thighs as her elbows rested on my shoulders. She'd lean toward me with plump lips whispering words of affection; her soft breasts pressed against my naked chest. The call girl became a necessity many a night, a pretence of love in my dark nights of the soul.

Smoking

It had been a while since I last saw Mum and Dad. They respected my space and my need for independence, but there was work I was unable to do and became frustrated with. They insisted on helping, arriving with their garden tools and homemade produce. Mum never arrived without a home-cooked meal.

"Hi, Mum," I said, as she walked up the ramp holding a dish covered by a tea towel. I was sure she'd be thinking, "*Povero figlio mio* (Poor son of mine)," at the sight of me, but she never let this on.

"Michelangelo." She said my full name when greeting me, and when offering food. "*Ho fatto i cannelloni* (I made cannelloni)."

"Oh, thanks Ma."

I turned to Dad. "Hi, Dad."

"Hello," he replied from the foot of the ramp. He squeezed the handle of the secateurs in my direction, mimicking scissors to cut my long hair. "You need a haircut, Michal."

"Tsk… Mick. *Lascia stare* (Leave him be)."

The two laboured: pruning, weeding and collecting the fallen twigs and leaf litter. I felt helpless and guilty. I kept thinking, *I once moved like them, working with gloves, raking and weeding; the sunlight hitting my brow as the sweat ran down my arms and chest, forever scratching at my legs from insect bites.*

I watched on from the patio as Dad tied the bundles of bracken with twine before the sunlight was lost. I lit up a cigarette and inhaled deeply, admiring my garden of Eden: a row of palm trees flanked the edges, wattles stood among them, ferns with curling fronds gathered at their base. Birds of paradise, with their striking flowers of of orange and purple stood out as the most beautiful. An archway with a climbing creeper led to a patch of green grass at the rear. *An ideal setting for a wedding, if I ever get married.* I exhaled a stream of smoke.

Dad looked up and frowned, his mouth turned down, shaking his head at me. I started smoking partly as an act of defiance. The silent gnawing of Dad's voice telling me to stop persisted, and it unsettled me. The more he voiced his disgust at my habit, the more I smoked to defy his authority. He had a hold on me that I struggled to shake off, as though I was still a kid. I wanted Dad to accept me as an adult, an independent person, and to respect my individuality, which I felt was denied for years. He smoked when I was young, Marcello smoked in his youth, so why couldn't I smoke now? I often wondered whether I smoked so I didn't feel so much like an outsider in my own family.

"Why you smoke, Michal?" asked Mum, clasping her hands.
   I shrugged my shoulders. "Because I want to, Mum."
   "Yeah?" she said, unconvinced.

"It relaxes me." I stared at the palm trees. "It makes me think of Nonno Joe." I turned to her. "I remember our holiday in Italy, I remember laughing with him. It makes me feel… good about myself."

One corner of her mouth turned up in an attempt to smile. "Michal, smoke is not good for you."

"You want to try, Mum?" I said, reaching out to her with the cigarette in hand.

"Michal, nooo."

"Go on."

She picked the cigarette off my fingers. "I hold like dis?" she said, demonstrating the grip.

"That's right."

She inhaled with caution, blowing puffs of smoke like a schoolgirl for the first time. She coughed after exhaling, "Yuk," she said, screwing up her face.

I laughed and she handed me back the cigarette.

"You know what?" she said.

"What?"

"Leah ring me last night."

My heart skipped a pulse. I steeled my body, anticipating what was to come. "Oh yeah?" I said, picking the bark of the twisted vine. "What did she say?"

"We talk for a long time," she said. "I ask her, 'You still like Michal?' She say 'Yes.'" Mum levelled her eyes at me. "She miss you, Michal."

I stared into the fernery, trying to distract myself from Leah's confession, yet I was delighted to hear it.

"Why you stop wid Leah?"

I paused, picking off large strips of bark. I avoided looking Mum in the eye. "I didn't want to stay together, Mum."

"Why?"

"Because… I want to be free. I want to… meet other people. I wanna be free." I turned to her. She looked at me with sympathy. Maybe she knew how it felt to be vulnerable with matters of the heart. Perhaps she hadn't had the luxury of freedom or choice that people of my generation enjoyed.

"Tsk. It's ok, Michal," she said, with a sigh. "*Vuoi che lavi i tuoi vestiti sporchi* (Do you want me to wash your dirty clothes?)."

"No, Mum, I'll do that – you've done enough for me today."

She headed off to the laundry despite my protest.

Crow Bar

It was late March, 1994, and the summer heat continued. Fresh faces moved in next door: Jase, Taz and Deano were all young students attending university, and musicians in a band.

Pearl Jam tunes carried into the dining room from their direction. I positioned my wheelchair close to the window, listening to the hypnotic beat, tapping away on the wooden table with a metal spoon. I turned up the volume on my stereo so Nirvana *Unplugged* could outdo my neighbours. With a VB stubby firmly between my thighs, I lifted the casters off the floor and balanced the wheelchair on its rear wheels, rocking back and forth to the rhythm. After a few more beers I lay back as far as I could against the plaster wall, my arms spread out and my head dropped to the side like dying Jesus on the cross.

"Mike." I turned down the stereo. "Hey, Mike?" Jase's voice called from over the fence.

I wheeled out onto the patio.

His head and arms leaned over the fence, "G'day mate."

"Hi Jase."

"You got Nirvana *Unplugged*?"

"Yeah, great album, hey?"

"Fucken oath it is."

"Let's do a swap. I'll borrow your Pearl Jam in exchange for my Nirvana?"

"Done," he said, brushing back his ponytail.

"Are you behaving yourself, Jase?"

"Yeah mate, always," he laughed, revealing the gap between his two front teeth. I leaned back on the wheelchair and lifted the front casters off the deck, holding the wheelie with firm hands.

"Ha! That's cool, man." Jase watched on as I rotated the chair in circles. "Hey, can I ask what happened?"

I stopped, dropping the casters onto the wooden deck with a thud. I moved forward to bridge the gap. "I had a car accident."

"Shit, man," he said with a shocked look. "How?"

I held onto the wheels. "I was a passenger in a car when the driver lost control." I gripped the tyres intensely. "I ended up sandwiched between a pole and the driver's seat next to me."

"Fuck man, that sucks."

"Yeah. Shit happens," I said, ripping off a leaf from the creeping vine.

He rubbed his chin. "So, what do you do?"

Sweat drops amassed in the middle of my chest and ran down my sides. "I'm a policeman." To confess was like cutting through layers of skin and muscle to reveal the innards, raw and exposed by fear of judgement. The beers had taken away some of that unease.

Jase's eyes widened, he smiled as if I was joking. "No you're not?"

"I had my car accident on duty."

"You're a copper?" he said with a surprised tone. "No shit."

"Yep." I dug my thumbnail into the palm of my hand, scratching it from left to right, "But not working at the moment." I picked off another leaf, ripping the organic matter into little pieces. I could see his disbelief.

"Shit, man."

"Hey," I pointed my finger toward him and started on the Pearl Jam song "Alive" – "Hey, I, o-oh, I'm still alive."

"Yeah man, sick." Jase watched on. He looked as though he was on the verge of asking me something but wasn't sure. "Hey… Taz, Deano and I are going out tonight to Crow Bar in the city. Do you wanna join us?"

"Um, yeah, why not?"

"Cool, we'll come over to pick ya up later."

"Cool," I replied.

"See ya later," he yelled as he climbed down the fence.

I pushed the chair through the kitchen door and spun on its rear wheels with the stubbie between my thighs. My spirit came alive, thinking about the night ahead. My arms and shoulders stretched at the hems of my t-shirt – I was feeling brave. I had been given an opportunity to revel into the night. The invitation was a validation of acceptance by the boys – an endorsement of my being, albeit in a wheelchair. I took a sip from the stubbie; I contemplated what could've been in my youth. I downed another mouthful. *I'm salvaging a thing of the past, acceptance of myself.* Back then, instead of going out and partying, I stayed in the safety and comfort of home, watching *Doctor Zhivago* and *Lawrence of Arabia* on Bill Collins's *Saturday Night Matinee*; Mum sitting in her chair with her *tazza di cafe* while Dad read the *Il Globo*.

It was my first night out since had I left the hospital. I arrived with Jase and the boys at a nightclub made of bluestone on King Street. The interior looked like a warehouse. The atmosphere inside was hot and electric, with the Seattle sound blasting from the wall speakers. I was more alive than ever before. The freedom and excitement I experienced defined me as one with my class of people. My hair, now down to neck length, concealed the silver earring in my left ear. I was introduced to Jase's friends, who sported a mix of hairstyles – one wore a semi-mohawk, another had dreadlocks, and a few wore blonde highlights.

The way they stared at me suggested they pitied me – or at least, that was what I thought.

A James Hetfield look alike with dreadlocks knelt beside me. "What do you do for work, mate?" he yelled above the music.

The question hit my chest like a hammer. *Fuck it; I'm gonna just say it.* "I'm a copper," I yelled back, intending to put venom in the answer. "I was injured on duty in a car accident." I expected a frosty reaction.

"No shit." He rested his hand on my wheel, interested in knowing more.

I suspected he'd taken an eccy from the look in his eye.

"How did it happen?"

I lifted my right leg and rested it on the footstool. "Well… we went to a 'shots fired' call out." Hetfield moved in closer as I told the story. "We were speeding when a car turned onto the road ahead of us. My driver tried to turn sharply to overtake and lost control." I dug my thumbnail into my ankle, feeling the tendon move back and forth. "And… I hit the guard rail in the median strip."

"Were you unconscious?"

"Nah, I was conscious." I looked him in the eye, "I wouldn't wish that pain on my worst enemy."

"Faaaark, at least you're alive man."

I stared at him, zombie-like, without feeling or thought. "Yeah, I guess so." I slapped my leg. "Hey, where's the toilet around here?"

Hetfield brushed his hair over his shoulders. "Man, they're upstairs."

I slumped my torso forward. "You're fucking kidding me."

"We can lift you, mate." Hetfield looked around. "I'll get the boys to give you a hand. Hey, Huddo!" he called out, lifting his beer at the semi-mohawk guy. "Give us a hand, mate. Lift our dude up the stairs to the dunnies."

Four came to my aid, Hetfield and the semi-mohawk holding either side of the chair, Jase and Deano behind.

"You know what you're doin, right?" Jase said.

"Yeah, mate. We've got him," Hetfield replied.

They lifted me, the chair rocking side to side, back and forth, up the stairs. I placed my hands on Huddo and Hetfield's shoulders to steady myself.

"Huddo, lift your side higher," Jase called out.

"Yeah, mate, I've got it," he replied.

The ordeal reminded me of being turned by the orderlies at the hospital. Girls stopped to give way, smiling at me with compassion. I smiled away, hot with embarrassment, sweat trickling from head to toe.

"Sorry, boys," I shouted.

"Nah, it's cool mate," Jase said. He sounded exhausted.

I reached the top, relieved not to have fallen off. The four boys stood aside, catching their breath.

"Thanks, fellas. Next shout is on me."

"You right to go in?" Jase asked.

"Mate, I don't expect you to hold it for me."

The boys laughed.

"Ha, you wish," he remarked, pushing the door open to aid my entry.

I forced the wheelchair past the door frame.

"You right, Mike?"

"Yeah, just need to get past this fuckin' door." I looked down and noticed the wheel rims sustaining scratch marks from my efforts.

Jase called out from behind the closed door, "I'll wait for ya outside."

My hands picked up wet, sticky toilet tissue as I pushed the wheels toward the cubicle. A tall, heavy-set guy stood in my way. I tried to move the chair around him. He stood firm, flicking his hands to rid of water; a few drops landed in my eye.

"You right, mate?" he asked.

"Yep, I'm right," I said, rubbing my eye with the back of my forearm.

He held the drunken stance, eyes heavy with sleaze. "Fuck, did you crawl to get up here?" He chuckled.

"Yep," I said with a sarcastic tone.

He stepped aside as I reached for the tap to wash off bits of paper and piss.

"What happened to ya?" He asked bluntly.

I stared back at him in the mirror. I noticed the Honda logo, with its iconic wings, on his t-shirt. I ran hot water over my hands. "I flew over the handlebars of my motorbike, a Fireblade."

His eyes widened, "Fair dinkum?" He brushed his hands against his jeans. "A 900cc?"

"Yep, lost it around the bend on the Great Ocean Road near Torquay. Over the railing and cliff, I fell."

"Fuck, man! How fast were ya going?"

I leaned back in my wheelchair. "Oh, about 120ks." I looked him in the eye. "And you know where I landed?"

He swayed, waiting for the finale.

"I landed on a whale carcass on the beach. The blubber broke my fall, but also broke my back."

He scratched his head, turned around and left.

I pushed the wheelchair toward the single cubicle. The door frame was too narrow for my wheelchair to pass, so I lifted my left leg and placed the heel onto the plastic seat. With my leg straightened, I stretched forward and pulled on the hem of my jeans. Under my jeans lay a latex urine bag held in place by Velcro straps. I unscrewed the valve on the bag's tube and released the stinking urine. The back of my leg started to cramp. "Faaark," I yelled as the urine spilt over my shoe. I capped off the leak and clawed at my ankle to get rid of the ache.

"You right, Mike?" Jase called out, standing one foot inside the bathroom.

"Yep," I yelled back. I didn't want to feel like a burden, so I kept up the pretence all was ok. I unscrewed the cap and pointed the bag toward the bowl, squeezing a steady stream of urine. "I won't be long," I called out to Jase. The sound of a precise trickle in the centre served as a temporary distraction from the pain.

"Hey, Mike," Jase yelled from across the crowded room, waving his hand. "Let's grab a drink."

Alcohol was the perfect remedy for nerve pain. "Excuse me," I said, making my way through the hordes. I felt the weight of their stares on me.

Jase went ahead of me, turning around now and then, "You right, mate?"

I nodded and pushed on till I reached the bar.

"What are ya havin'?" Jase asked, tucking his hair behind his ears.

"Scotch and Coke." I handed him a twenty-dollar note.

He brushed off my offer. "Nah mate, my shout this round."

Scotch and Coke reminded me of Leah. On our first date, she drank Scotch and Coke. Even though I didn't drink at the time, I ordered one too, to impress her.

Like Moses parting the Red Sea, Jase ushered the crowd aside to make a path for me. "Outta the way, guy in a wheelchair coming through."

The crowd watched me push my chair like I was a show freak. We settled at a table close to the stage, my chest thumping from the beat of the bass speakers. I lifted my right foot onto the edge of the dance floor; the left foot remained placed on the footplate. I tried to conceal my left leg by placing my right leg over it – the pee bag took the shape of the Hindenburg when full, its weight heavy as a brick.

I saw her silhouette against the strobe lights, a Gauguin painting come to life with sparkles of coloured light bouncing around her. Catching my eye, she smiled, and I smiled back. My stomach jumped. She raised her arms, swaying her hips in a tight black dress like a Latin dancer.

Jase leaned over my shoulder, "I know her." He fixed his hair into a ponytail. "She was a swimwear model."

The smile I thought had been directed at me was cast in doubt. I cursed myself for being such a fool. She moved off the stage and headed toward us.

"Hi, Jase," she said, embracing him. She flicked a glance at me and smiled.

"How are ya?" Jase asked.

"I'm good, thanks," she said. "You?"

"I'm doing great, thank you for asking," he replied, mimicking Jim Carey's Ace Ventura.

She turned to me again, "Hi."

"Oh, this is Mike," Jase said.

I extended my hand in greeting. "Hi."

"I'm Bridget." She played with her necklace. "How do you know, Jase?"

"I live next door to him."

"Oh. Is Jase a good neighbour?" She asked with sarcasm.

"Ah, yeah." I looked at Jase. "But he can be a pain in the arse."

Bridget broke out into laughter.

"You liar!" Jase retorted, trying not to smile.

I caught Bridget's eye. "Nah, he's a good guy."

The conversation between Bridget and me went on longer than I anticipated, much to my delight. A connection was developing.

Come Out and Play by The Offspring commenced. "Oh, I love this song." She reached out and grabbed my hand. "Come dance with me?"

"Nah, I can't." I looked pointedly at my feet.

"Oh, come on." She walked backwards, leading me by the hand as I steadied the wheelchair. I turned around to see Jase watching us.

"I can't get up," I called out. "There are steps to the dance floor."

She flicked her hand to dismiss my concern. "We can dance here."

Though I tried, I couldn't keep up with her. There was magic within her, a magnetism drawing me close as she swayed her hips. I was on a high, almost having to pinch myself that this was real.

"Let's get a drink," she commanded.

We moved to a dark vacant corner, talking and drinking, the cosmos working in my favour.

She asked the inevitable question, "What happened to you, if you don't mind me asking?"

I took a drag on a cigarette. "I had a car accident, nearly died." I exhaled slowly, watching the smoke rise to blend with the flashing strobe lights. "I was on police duty."

Bridget dropped her glass of beer, "Shit!" The contents rushed over my face and clothes. "Oh shit, sorry."

I wiped my eye with the bottom of my shirt, the yeasty smell settling on my nose. "It's ok," I said, trying to lessen the awkwardness.

"I'm so sorry." She clumsily patted down the wet spots on my t-shirt. "You, ok? Can I get you a towel from the bar?"

I looked her in the eye. "Hey, don't worry about it."

"It just slipped out of my hand. How embarrassing."

"About time I had a shower anyway."

Bridget laughed and I felt my confidence growing. Our eyes locked, morphing into a powerful attraction. She leaned over and kissed me. Our lips opened, and we continued kissing with our tongues. I pulled out of the kiss and reached for her hand, inviting her to sit on my lap.

She laughed. "No, I'm too heavy."

"No, you're not." I held her hand. "I'll prove it to you."

She turned to assume the sitting position. As she lowered herself down, I positioned one arm under her legs, the other around her waist.

"No, I'm too heavy!" she cried.

I lifted her onto my lap. She shrieked, holding me tight

around the shoulders and neck. She paused to catch my eye, "I have a boyfriend, you know?"

"No, I didn't know that," I replied with a smile, gently playing with her hair. The heat intensified as we kissed. My hand moved up her stockings and onto her soft inner thigh.

"BRIDGET?" A woman's voice called out. I looked up to find a girl with a scowl fast approaching. She grabbed Bridget by the arm and pulled her off me. "What are you doing?"

"What?" Bridget protested. "We're just chatting."

"We're going home," she said, marching off into the crowd, dragging Bridget by the hand. I followed Bridget's every step until I lost sight of her.

That experience ignited an explosive passion for wanting more of the same. I didn't know what day of the week it was, as long as the momentum of fun and frivolity continued. I came alive, carrying on with my antics, escorting ladies onto my lap, feeling brave and shaking with excitement. I wanted to make the most of my second chance; a personal protest against the fuckery life had dealt me. I salvaged dignity from drinking, freeing myself from the torment of disability. The liaisons with strangers fed my adrenaline. And with it, I feared so much.

One night I awoke on the sofa to the sound of the telephone. The light emanating from the TV cleared my blurry vision as I reached for the receiver. "Hello?"

I heard her exhaling what I imagined was a steady stream of cigarette smoke. It was a familiar sound.

"Hi," Leah said in a sombre voice.

I could tell that she'd been crying.

"Hi, Leah," I said, serious to match her mood. "You ok?"

She drew on the cigarette and exhaled. "Oh, I'm feeling

wonderful." A long pause followed. "I need to talk. Can I come over?"

"What, now?" I said with surprise. I didn't want to see her, yet my heart flirted with the idea of reliving the good times.

"Is that, ok?"

"Yeah, ok."

My heart leapt at her knock. I opened the front door, and there she stood, eyes dry but swollen from crying. "Hi." She wore a green shirt I had given her and long forgotten about.

"Hi, Leah." I opened the door wider. "Come on in."

She sat on the couch, staring at the coffee table where empty beer stubbies sat neatly in a row.

"Would you like a drink?"

"Do you have red wine?"

"I do."

"Thank you." She reached into her bag. "Do you mind if I smoke?"

"No, it's ok."

The two of us settled on the couch. The light from the TV set the mood.

"What happened to us?" she said, facing me.

My face tightened, and my throat began to dry. "I don't know." The middle of my forehead tightened. "What do you want me to say?"

"Why don't you love me?"

I struggled to find the words. I felt like I'd lost my wits. "I… don't know, Leah."

She leant forward, flicking the cigarette into the ashtray. "Why can't we be together?" Her eyes began to moisten. "When you left me..." The tears, blackened with mascara, rolled down her cheeks.

"Hey, come here." I wrapped my arms around her. "I'm sorry." It was a long embrace. She lifted her head to meet me at eye level. She leaned forward, and we kissed. The familiarity of her lips and the way she moved brought back memories of a love that once was.

We stopped. The ties that brought us together were no longer. I had become a stranger to her since the accident. I was a new person.

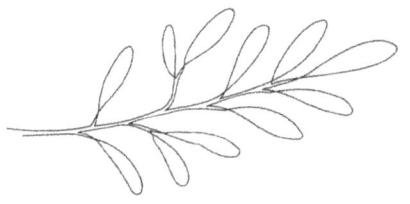

"That's My Boy"

I woke up one morning in April 1994 to answer a phone call.
"Hello?"

"Michael Tarully, is it?" A raspy voice said.

Sheesh. My name is Tarulli, like Tabouli. The formality of his tone made me suspicious.

"Yes, speaking."

"District Commander Baker here… how are ya, young man?"

I stared at the blank wall with my throat tightening. "I'm good, Sir."

"Good, good. Listen… we think you are best to come back to Heidelberg Police Station. We can set you up at reception with a desk. How do you feel about that?"

"Ah…" My head was consumed with uncertainty.

"We're all looking forward to having you back… Ah!" I imagined him scratching his head. "You can start on light duties." The delivery was unconvincing, like he was selling a half-baked muffin.

I felt obliged to answer in the affirmative. "That would be good, Sir." I was too weak to speak my truth, overcome by a fear of those like him. "Yeah, I look forward to it."

"Ok, let me know when you want to start."
"Yes, Sir."

After our conversation, I wheeled onto the back patio next to the creeping vine. I bent down with folded arms pressing against my stomach. I replayed the phone conversation in my head. I doubted my ability to work again.

I stared down onto the brick pavement below and watched an ant moving back and forth, round and round in circles, with his antennae going crazy. *Maybe he's lost, or injured, separated from the others, considered an outcast. He's like me.*

I wasn't ready to wear the blue uniform again. I doubted I would ever be.

Wayne returned my police hat, along with my utility belt – which had been cut clean in half by the trauma surgeons.

"That's what's left of it from the emergency ward," he said, handing it over to me.

I didn't understand. *Why the utility belt?* But I never asked, assuming he gave it to me as a memento.

"I don't want to go back to Heidelberg."

"Hmm, why?"

"I don't feel good about it." I let out a heavy sigh. "It's like returning to a nightmare."

"You can work with me." There was a calmness in his voice. "We have a good crew in my department." Wayne had been transferred to a plain clothes division performing surveillance work.

I looked at him with some optimism, "Can I think about it?"

He placed his hand on my shoulder. "Sure."

The police psychologist called, requesting my attendance in her office to discuss a return to work, or so I thought. The hairs on my arms bristled as I locked eyes with the psychologist.

"Hello," she said, examining me through her spectacles. She extended her arm in the direction of my chair. "Please take a seat."

But I'm already sitting. I positioned my wheelchair in front of her with nervous anticipation. She held a deadpan face. It was the same look as Mrs Prior from my primary school. Mrs Prior whipped my hand with the end of a thin metal ruler for playing football in the classroom with José, a Chilean immigrant I had befriended. I had been showing him how to kick and handpass the football; she was unimpressed. She also once instructed me to write "I shall not ride my bike on school grounds" on the blackboard one hundred times.

"How do you feel going back to work?" the psychologist asked.

I shrugged my shoulders, "A little uncomfortable."

"Why do you feel uncomfortable?"

"I'm not sure what to expect… like… how are they going to treat me?"

She peered over her glasses, "Who do you mean when you say 'they'?"

I cleared my throat. "People at work, those in charge."

"Why do you think that?"

"Coz… of what happened. And I'm sort of different now."

She held her pen above the folder, scribbling away. I scratched at my palm, anticipating the next question. She took a deep breath through her nostrils and looked up at me. "How do you feel about meeting Mark Moyle?"

The mention of his name lit the fuse, sparking an explosion of nerves throughout my body. "I don't want to see him."

"Why?" she asked casually.

"Because I'm angry with him," and scared, which I didn't admit to her.

She took off her reading glasses. "What about Mark?" she snapped. "Have you thought about how he's feeling."

I straightened up and looked into the eyes of the rising cobra. The crown of thorns tightened around my forehead. "I don't want to see him."

I thought about our meeting long after. I figured she was angling for me to accept his apology. If I did so, Moyle would be off the hook, he'd have a free pass to get on with his life. No, I wanted him to feel the burden of what I was going through. If I was going down, he was going down with me. The meeting with the psychologist was the first and last.

That night, I took to a bottle of scotch. The warm memories greeted me with glee as the night wore on; like when I ran to the corner shop pretending to be the sprinter Darren Clark with Dad's change in my hand for his Peter Stuyvesants. I'd throw my hands up in the air in victory over an imaginary finish line.

I swallowed prescribed painkillers with my scotch to dream up more memories as "1979" by The Smashing Pumpkins played on the stereo. Denise Keogh, a Marcia Brady lookalike from primary school, pinned me against the fence and laid her lips against mine in a game of kiss-chasey. I laughed out loud thinking about it, trying to keep upright as I began leaning to the side.

I visualised Caroline's smile, blue eyes and golden hair. I imagined her and me making out; the inner chatterbox reminded me of what could've been. I swallowed the remaining liquid and slammed the glass hard onto the table. I wanted to return to the sweet spot of nostalgia. At three in the morning, I picked up the phone to make an international call to my Uncle Nic, Mum's older brother. I wanted to reminisce about our tour of Italy in 1978. I wanted the spirit of Nonno Joe to come alive. Uncle Nic sounded like him when he spoke, so he was the next best thing.

"I have an N Antonino in Pago Veiano, Italy?" said the international operator.

"Yeah, yeah, that's the one."

"Connecting you now." The long dial tones commenced.

I blew a raspberry.

"Pronto?" said the voice on the other end.

He sounds like Uncle Nic.

"Ciao Zio," I said in my Auslo-Italian accent. "*Sono Michelangelo, figlio di Rufina.*"

"*Ciao, come stai, Michelangelo* (How are you)?" He replied.

After five minutes of conversation, the person on the other end proved not to be my uncle, but Mum's cousin Nic, the pastry chef. The name Nicolo (Nic) was popular in the village. I struggled with my drunken vocabulary to continue our conversation, and so to save further embarrassment, I politely ended the phone call, wishing him luck.

I woke up the next morning to the sound of the garbage truck's high-pitched hydraulic arms. It resembled a power drill boring into my skull. To ease the pain, I imagined the ethanol sludge seeping out of my head. Then a blackbird decided to chirp outside my window. I imagined him calling, "Get up, you lazy shit."

I found the urinal lining tangled around my legs. I opened an eye, and like most mornings, the sight of my wheelchair reminded me it was no dream. My left quadricep began to twitch as I tried to remove the lining. This muscle flicker was noticeably large. The hangover pain was cancelled out by the anticipation of the next muscle jerk as I lay there waiting. Many mornings, muscle twitches fired on and off from both legs, which excited me. My long-lost friend was coming back to life. The secret joy extended to the self-belief of one day walking again.

Each morning I'd rest on my side and move my lower leg forward an inch or two, pretending to kick a footy. "That's my boy," I'd say. I'd lift the bedsheets and observe the lower legs move slightly. I'd push down my right leg, pretending to squash a Coke can, imagining the feel and sound of the crunch I knew from when I was a kid wearing Lee jeans and Converse sneakers.

Wheels

The opportunity to work in the plain clothes division appealed to me so I chose to work with Wayne as an analyst-in-training at Transit Patrol. Our desks abutted, though mine faced the office of Senior Sergeant Caughey, or "Corgi" as I called him, much to Wayne's amusement. Alec Caughey had a clear view of me from behind his glass-partitioned office, which worried me – I held a suspicion of anyone at and above the rank of Sergeant. When we crossed paths, we talked about footy – either the Police Football League or AFL – which allayed my fear of him. He knew I played football with the VFA club Box Hill Mustangs.

"Joining us to watch the footy, Wheels?" he asked.

"Yeah, I'm up for it." I was always keen to lend a hand with the Central Districts Demons on a Wednesday afternoon.

"Wheels, I need you to help me out," Corgi said during half-time, the magnetic whiteboard in hand. "Where do you think we're going wrong?"

I picked up the magnets from the board. "Well, I think these guys need to spread the ball out onto the wings, the opposition is slow on the outside. So, if we move Macca on one wing and Clarko on the other," I placed the magnets down, "we can get 'em with our speed when we break."

He grinned. "Yeah, yeah, that's a great idea," he said.

It warmed me knowing I meant so much to him and the team for two hours that afternoon.

I wore my multicoloured hippie top and denim jeans to work. My hair was long enough to need a hair tie. A wristband made of seashells became a favourite accessory, along with a jade pendant worn around my neck. I progressed from two hours to four hours of work a day. Still, I'd look up from my computer screen to catch gazes fixed on me. They'd break away pretending to do something else: one officer, chewing gum, would look down to pick up a report from his desk, another would arch his back with arms raised in the air to imitate a stretch.

Sergeant Danny Morgan approached me one day. "Wheels, how are you feeling today?"

"Yeah, good," I said, puffing out my cheeks with lips pressed together.

"We've got a big game this week, play'n the top side, Southern Bears. I'd like you to give a pre-game rev-up for the boys. Would ya like to do that?"

I nodded my head. "Yeah, ok."

"Great, thanks." He turned to walk off but stopped and faced me again. "Hey, you don't mind me asking." He folded his arms against his barrel chest. "What happened with the car accident you were involved in?"

I dug my thumbnail into the palm of my opposite hand, obliged to retell the story, much to my annoyance.

"Mate, you've come through, that's the main thing. Could've been a lot worse."

That line again, could've been worse. "Yeah, I know." The effort of having to act like I was thankful to be alive felt like a load of horse shit had just dropped onto me. I looked at the clock. "Shit, is that the time?" I turned to the computer screen. "Gotta finish these stats, pronto."

Ten minutes later I placed my bag on the back of my wheelchair, ready to go.

"Hey Wheels?" called out Nash, an analyst who sat near my desk.

"Yes?"

"What's that?" he said, pointing to my wristband. He looked at Wayne, smirking.

Wayne flashed his eyes at me, smiling nervously, not giving Nash the pleasure.

"Aah, it's called a bracelet!" I replied in a sarcastic tone.

"Are you coming out?" he said, laughing.

"Don't worry, Nash – if I was, you'd be safe. You're not my type."

A chorus of laughter erupted around the office.

That night I went out with the boys, drinking at a Bourke Street nightclub. Jase waved his arm at me. "Mike, let's go home."

"Nah, I'm stayin'."

He brushed his hair to the side, looking at me with doubt. "C'mon man, Taz and Deano are going home."

I looked toward the exit and saw the guys waiting for me. "Yeah, nah, I'm stayin'."

I continued drinking, waiting for a girl to notice me, to carry on with me into the early hours of the morning. I knocked on the glass enclosure, drawing the attention of Sal, the DJ. He took off his headphones.

"Play 'Blister in the Sun'," I yelled. Sal nodded his head. An hour later, I squeezed through the crowd using my arms and shoulders, knocking on the windowpane harder. "Play 'Killing In The Name'," I yelled.

Sal pressed his ear to the glass pane.

"PLAY 'KILLING IN THE NAME'!"

He gave a thumbs-up, and my merry night continued. I lifted myself onto a barstool, "Scotch and coke, thanks." A sharp pain encircled my hips as the catheter jammed up against the buttoned jeans. I undid the top button to give my gut some breathing space; and waited for anyone who cared to converse with me. I fidgeted with the paper napkin, punched holes in the beer coaster, and for good measure wrapped the plastic straw around my finger till it numbed. The music stopped and the lights came on. I knew it was closing time – five in the morning.

"Ok, time to leave buddy," the security guy said, pointing me to the exit.

"Yep, just finishing my last drop." I gulped down the remaining liquor and slammed down the glass.

I emerged from the hidden den. "Hey there," I called out to a group of girls. I swayed on my wheelchair, trying to remain upright. "Where are we off to?"

They turned and giggled.

I made my way to the traffic lights. I placed the brake on, reached under my wheelchair and unfastened the Velcro strap to retrieve a can of Jim Beam. I leaned against the traffic signal and drank slowly. I felt the vibration of the pedestrian traffic signal rattling against my spine, intervals of quick and slow bursts. The flashing red man looked at me. "What are you doing to yourself?" he asked.

I hunched over, the guilt of my errant ways came to the fore. I looked up again, and the green man shone. "Go all out," he said.

"Yeah, why the fuck not," I called out, raising the can in the air to him. I sat up straight, feeling brave, and emptied the can into my mouth.

I detoured to a nearby lane, out of sight, and doubled over, throwing up. Each guttural heave blurred my vision. Nonno Joe stood in front of me, wearing his fedora and bomber jacket. He gestured with pressed fingertips, waving them at me. "*Cosa fai* (What are you doing)?"

I loosened the valve of my leg bag and watched urine trickle between the bluestone cracks, too ashamed to meet his eyes.

I waved my hand at each passing taxi and cursed them for failing to stop.

About an hour had passed when a police van pulled up in front of me. The window wound down. "Mick Tarulli!" the female officer called out. Her face was familiar. I couldn't remember her name or where I knew her from.

"G'day, fellas," I bellowed.

"What are you up to?" she said, sounding like a disappointed mother.

"I'm going home… I think."

"C'mon, we'll take you."

The warmth of belonging still burned. I was helped into the back of the van, seated on a raised metal strip with the smell of puke and petroleum. I held onto the wheelchair to prevent it from moving about. *We've been bad tonight my friend.* We came to a halt outside my home. She stood behind the wheelchair as I slid my bum over from metal to cushion.

"You okay?" she asked.

"Yep," I said, wheeling away towards the front door.

"Look after yourself, Mick."

I turned around, "Yep, I'll try." I fumbled at the keyhole, aware they were watching me. I opened the door, turned around and gave a thumbs-up. I pushed past the front door and rolled into the bedroom with my torso leaning over the side. I was alone again, and the quiet reality settled in. I reflected on the night; fury seized my heart. I ripped off my top, and with pen in hand scribbled foul language in the form of a journal. The word "FUCK" was used a lot.

I wheeled onto the back patio as the cold air crawled over my chest and back. I grabbed the cigarette wedged behind my ear and lit up. I rolled forward and slumped against the wooden post, the vine nudging my cheek. The sparrows jumped from branch to branch, chirping in unison. The birds of paradise stood proud at the foot of the palm trees. I looked up at the morning sky and opened my arms out wide, asking God, "What's become of me?"

He didn't answer.

The birds continued with their melody. I blew smoke in steady streams toward the heavens, the rising sun casting an amber glow against the clouds. *How strange. I've succumbed to darkness amid the colour and earthly sounds.*

Deep Blue

I wheeled out of the office with the file on my lap. I felt nervous. The effort of pushing became harder, the wheelchair taking on a tank-like feel. A search warrant was required for authorisation by an officer. That officer was Superintendent Canning. I was told he was a difficult communicator going by his brash manner.

I entered his office and greeted his assistant. "Hiya, Maria."

"Hi, Michael. *Come stai* (How are you)?"

"*Bene grazie, e tu* (I'm good thanks, you)?"

"*Bene, bene* (Good, good)."

Maria's parents were also Italian. Born and raised in Broadmeadows, she understood my stories of growing up in Australia as children of migrants.

"You've come to see Mr Canning?"

"Yep, he's expecting me."

She picked up the phone. "Constable Tarulli is here." She placed the phone down. "He's ready to see you."

I wheeled through the door with caution, steadying the file on my lap. "Hi, Sir."

He adjusted his tie with an outstretched neck. "Constable Tarully is it?" The weight of his tone pressed against me.

"Yes, Sir." *It's Tarulli, like Tabouli.* "Sir, I have a warrant for you to sign off on." I handed him the report. "The informant is reliable in my opinion."

He flipped the page over. "Is the suspect considered dangerous?"

"No, Sir."

He penned his signature at the bottom of the page and placed the file on the desk. He leaned back in his spring-loaded chair with hands behind his head. "You need a shave and a haircut, young fella. You look like you don't want to be here." He leaned forward, placing his fingertips against each other as if praying for my release. "Young fella, you've got to ask yourself, is this job right for you?"

I was surprised by his abruptness. My skin prickled.

"You know you can always go to university, to start over again?"

I picked up the file from his desk with trembling fingers.

"Would you consider that?"

I sat up with my chest out, nostrils flaring with each breath. "With all respect Sir, that's for me to decide." I hit the cardboard folder upright on the desk to bring the paper back in order, all the while staring at him with steeled eyes, channelling my mother's fiery temperament. I turned to leave and hit the corner desk with the footplate, leaving a mark on the corner. "Oh… sorry about that." Redness and heat burned beneath my skin.

"See you, Michael," Maria called out as I wheeled past.

I turned to Maria and offered a strained smile, steadying the warrant on my lap. She knew I was upset.

Corgi walked out of his office as I wheeled to my desk. Our eyes locked, communicating without words. He frowned. "You right, Wheels?"

I glanced over at Wayne who sat at his desk with coffee in hand. I sighed, "Yeah, just tired, boss." I scratched the side of my nose, avoiding eye contact.

"Why don't you go home, get some rest," he said, sliding a piece of creased paper between his finger and thumb.

"Yeah, might just do that." I threw the file onto the desk. "The warrant's signed, boss."

"I'll give that to the boys. Just close off the computer and sign out." He continued walking with his back turned to me. "See you tomorrow morning, Wheels."

Wayne placed his coffee mug down. "You ok?"

I shrugged my shoulders. "The job's fucked." I said, using the common police shorthand to convey my frustration.

He laughed at my retort, then looked at me with concern.

"What do you think of Canning?" I asked him.

"Mmm, he's odd. Why?"

I raised my eyebrows, shaking my head. The burn still coursed through my body.

He chuckled. "I've heard not very nice things about him."

I peeled off my top, the sweat streaming down the side of my singlet. "Do they say he's a wanker?"

Wayne burst out laughing. "Did you have a run-in with him?"

I picked up a sharpened pencil and stabbed at the file.

"What happened?"

I dropped the pencil and leaned back, folding my arms against my chest, staring ahead and listening to the rough office noise behind me. "I don't know anymore." I looked at Wayne. "I just gotta get away from it all."

"What do you mean?"

I glanced over my shoulder before I could answer. "I just feel like a nothing person... like... no one sees me... like I'm a ghost." The tears were on the cusp of spilling over.

"Don't be silly," he smiled with effort. "You're Michael, you matter to me, and to your family and friends." He picked at his fingernail, "Hmm?"

I planted my face in the palm of my hands, moving them up and down to remove the itch that crept over. "Ok, I'm done. I'm going home. Gotta catch the 3:20 train."

The exchange with Canning played over and over in my head that night. I listened to *Deep Blue Day* by Brian Eno on an endless loop, spinning the wheelchair in circles. I picked up my full glass and swirled around the scotch and ice with crushed codeine mixed in. "I love you." I swallowed the liquid. The dark shadow came to remind me that family and friends were slipping away. I replayed my recent conversation with Chris Haggarty in my head – he was moving to Western Australia.

"Mate, I need a change," he said, exhausted at the thought of telling me. "I feel like I'm abandoning you."

"Nah mate, don't be stupid. I support you." I placed my arm around his shoulder. "Do what makes you happy."

He turned to me with a sad look.

"Seriously, go and follow your heart," I said, slapping my hand on his back.

In only a year I had lost Marcello and Chris to their wives and Scotty Hepburn, a next-door neighbour I grew up with, died in a car accident. Scotty was like a younger brother to me, a redheaded kid with freckles and a big-hearted smile. I thought of the summer days he and I spent playing cricket on the driveway and kicking the footy on the road.

I lay my head sideways on the dining table, staring at Mirella's blue oriental vase on the floor. The same vase I broke into pieces a few years ago and glued back together in haste for fear of Mirella's wrath. The finished product looked so good I thought she wouldn't find out.

A few days later, Mirella stared at the vase while eating at the dining table.

"Is that?" She dropped the fork and squinted. "Did you break that?" She said, pointing at it. I had kept the repaired vase ever since.

My vision blurred through tears. I imagined myself sinking further into the deep blue. *Let me go down; the silence is bliss here, and the sensation is a lot cooler. Carry me away tidal current to wherever you please, away from the madness above.*

I awoke with my head pounding from the ringing telephone. The answering service activated, "G'day! How are you? ... Oh, that's good... Got ya! I'm not home at the moment so leave a message after the beep." I lay on the floor where I'd slept, listening for the caller's message.

"G'day, Wheels, Alec Caughey here. Can you pick up the phone?"

His voice sounded like a screeching violin. I slumped my carcass onto the wheelchair; sunlight shone into my eyes through the curtain edges. I scratched my head trying hard to get back to the living, my back remembering every inch of the timber floor.

I wheeled to the toilet and released the valve to my urinal bag. The cloudy piss stank of stale cheese as it poured into the porcelain bowl. As the last drops emptied, I closed off the valve and wheeled over to the bathroom. I stared into the mirror. My eyes were bloodshot, the veins under my skin bright blue. The stranger looked back, with no expression and no soul. "Who are you?" I asked. The absence of identity left me vulnerable. I focused on the black pinhole in the centre of my eye; the silence became deafening. The sound of my inhale and exhale had me in a trance; like I was stuck between the present and the afterlife. *Am I real? Is this all real?* I hit my head against the mirror. Strands of hair crunched between glass and skull. I thought of Nonno Joe, gesturing at me with pressed fingertips, asking, "What the hell are you doing to yourself?"

I pressed play on the answering machine.

"G'day, Wheels, Alec Caughey here. Can you pick up the phone?" A long pause followed. "Give me a call when you get a chance."

I wheeled away, hearing the crackle of the receiver closing down on the cradle.

"How would I know if he's suicidal?" Corgi said, failing to hang up the phone properly. "If he's suicidal, then what can I do about it?"

I replayed the message to see if I heard correctly. I rubbed my head with both hands, driving out whatever demon resided there. Corgi's comment was further proof I was a burden to the Police Force. I wheeled to my place of comfort, the sofa, and lay there hugging a cushion like it was a teddy bear. I squeezed hard, feeling the nerves slip from my chest like drops of sorrow.

Yarran Dheran

It was spring, a Sunday, and I wanted to see Mum and Dad, to surprise them. I felt another strange and exciting twitch of the entire right quadriceps, from near its origin in the hip area to the knee cap. At other times, subtle contractions occurred in sections of each quad muscle. Each sensation sent a streak of hope, reinforcing my pledge to walk again. I kicked my lower left leg forward, watching the bedsheets move like an ocean wave. My leg moved about four inches. My right leg was getting stronger. "C'mon, don't lag behind your brother," I said to my left leg. I looked over at the wheelchair next to my bed. He was waiting for me. I sat up. With my right hand holding the frame of the wheelchair, my left lay firm on the mattress for support as I momentarily bore body weight on my right leg to pivot onto the chair's cushion. I called this move the "bent-over stance with a forty-five-degree knee bend twist"; a 7 out of 10 on a judge's scorecard. I repeated the sequence for the shower cubicle, the toilet, and in and out of the driver's seat. I didn't fear getting behind the steering wheel; I could use my right foot to push the accelerator and pump the brakes. The liberty of driving had never felt so good.

From the shower chair, I shoved my bony arse onto the parked wheelchair. I quickly wrapped the towel around my waist to conceal the disfigurement. I looked at the foggy mirror with water dripping off my hair and chin. From my neck to my navel, I stared at the line of scarring. I still found it hard to believe the transformation of my body, from athletic to busted-up bag of bones and tissue.

I drove to the old home and transferred from the driver's seat to the wheelchair. The anticipation of seeing their faces hurried my action as I wheeled my way from the driveway to the side gate, and through to the rear of the house. I reached the first flight of steps, got off the chair and placed my backside on the step. I moved up onto the second step, hauling the chair after me in such a way to keep the cushion stable. Dad watched on from his seat at the kitchen table. He stood up to get a closer look; his eyes widened with surprise. I moved onto the third and final step with the chair in tow.

Mum walked over to the door. "Michelangelo!" she called out, placing her hands to her chest, *"Ti aiuterò* (I'll help you)!"

"No Ma, I can do this myself," I said, panting. "The jeans were made for this sort of stuff."

"Michal don't hurt yurself," Dad called out.

"I'm ok."

"Stai attento (Be careful)," Mum implored.

I looked up at her, smiling. "I'm ok, Mum, *sono forte* (I am strong)."

She opened the flywire door for me to enter. "Tsk, I know, *sei forte* (you're strong)," she said, with her Neapolitan accent.

I reached my favourite chair and executed my bent-over stance move, lowering myself onto it. "Ahh, there."

Mum and Dad looked at me with surprise, stunned by my performance.

I laughed. "If Jesus can walk on water, the least I can do is pirouette on one leg from chair to chair."

Mum held her hands to her chest and looked up to the heavens, mumbling a prayer. Dad held his stare as his lips quivered and tears gathered at the corner of his eyes. There was a deathly silence amidst their joy, knowing I'd overcome great obstacles. They had known for a while that my legs had regained a little movement and strength, but witnessing this transfer was a first.

I sat with my back against the wall, breathing a sigh of relief. "Hi, Mum."

Mum embraced me and kissed me on the cheek three times.

I turned to Dad and acknowledged him with a nod. "Dad."

His eyes were streaming with tears. "Ello Michal," he mumbled.

The smell of fresh-brewed coffee and Mum's cooking calmed the senses.

I talked with Dad about footy and politics; with Mum, it was mostly gardening and cooking. She gave me instructions on treating diseased plants at home, and how to prune the rose bush. And she offered tips on dough kneading and my attempts at homemade gnocchi – the trouble was, I'd decorate the kitchen and my clothes with excess flour as opposed to adding enough to the dough.

"Michelangelo, *hai mangiato* (have you eaten)?"

"Yes Mum, don't worry about me."

"Ow's work, Michal?" Dad asked.

I scratched at the back of my neck. "It's ok." I was unable to look him in the eye.

"The bosses good to you?"

I darted my eyes at Dad. "Some are," I said, rubbing my nose. I turned away, staring at the tall eucalypt, visualising myself buried in his trunk. I wanted to change the conversation. "Not a very nice day, is it?" I said. The sun tried hard to break through the clouds.

Dad sliced the hardened bread in half. "Michal, please cut your hair."

I took delight in pulling the strands to reveal their length.

"You look like a billy goat, Michal."

"I like billy goats, Dad."

He ignored my stare, squeezing lemon wedges over his fish instead. I rolled my thumbs over one another waiting for a follow-up comment.

"You speak to Mirella?" Dad said.

"No."

"You hear from Marcello?"

"No."

"You been drinking again. I can see."

I turned my palms up in the air. "Why do you always say that?" I shook my head at him.

He chewed away on his bread and fish. "You look tired, Michal."

I rubbed my forehead vigorously with both hands. "Listen, I just want to enjoy my time with you Dad." I stared at him, "So don't push it."

The sound of the oven fan blasting hot air against the tempered glass became noticeably louder.

"Mick, *lascialo stare* (leave him be)," Mum said, rubbing the back of her neck.

The aroma of homemade lasagna clashed with the odour of garlic and cooked fish.

"Who are you making lasagna for, Mum?"

"A friend de Marcello."

"What for? Mum, you always make lasagna for people you don't know. What do they do for you?"

"I know… but… what can I say when they ask for lasagna?"

Dad shook his head in agreement with me as he chewed on his meal.

"Anyway, how have ya been, Ma?"

"Tsk, not good. I'm really upset with your father." She darted her eyes at Dad.

I knew better than to ask questions.

"I tell him to use de kitchen downstairs to clean and grill de fish. I get upset when he not listen to me."

Dad scowled at Mum, anger rising in him.

I'd witnessed the scene before and knew how it would end. Like a paper towel, my flesh absorbed their hostility. I grew up listening to Mum's tears as a child. I consoled her in my youth, feeling the very pain she was going through. I counselled her, "Try not to get upset," or "Just ignore him," knowing it was easier said than done. Mum heaped all of her burden and frustration onto me. Perhaps there were hidden secrets, a lingering pain. I didn't want to acknowledge the feelings of resentment toward Mum during these tirades, but that is what I harboured inside. So I willingly listened to her cry for help, to ease her pain. And Dad proved difficult to reason with. "Leave Mum alone," I'd implore. "Stop upsetting her." My words fell silent with him. I remembered standing defiantly in front of him as Mum stood behind me; the weight of his anger under the influence of alcohol rushed at me as I stood with clenched fists. Perhaps he, like Mum, was afflicted with a hidden pain he dared not reveal. I suspected the trauma of the past, war followed by famine, was hidden deep in their consciousness.

I stared at Dad, shaking my head. I twisted the paper napkin around my index finger to fight off the anger building up. I looked up to the heavens, "Why do I bother?"

"Michelangelo. No get upset," Mum said.

"No, I'm upset because I want to relax and enjoy myself when I visit, but you two never make it easy… always arguing… it's always the same." I hammered my fist onto the table, spilling Dad's espresso over the edge of his cup. "I hate my life!"

"Michelangelo, please," Mum said, her voice quivering.

I turned away, staring at the gum tree, feeling the weight of their eyes on me. The blood vessels pressed hard against my skull. The tree had never looked better to be buried in. "Wish I died that day."

The air turned cold. I turned to face them, unable to maintain eye contact, wishing to swallow back the spoken words.

"Michelangelo." Mum placed a hand over her forehead. "Please no say this."

Dad sat with clasped hands, staring at me like a cat, one eye wide open and the other half closed, as if to say, "I think I know what's happening but I'm not quite sure what to make of it."

I lurched forward on my right leg to sit on the moving wheelchair. "Gotta go now. I… need to get some rest."

"Michal." Mum sighed, rubbing the backs of her hands.

I bummed my way down the steps again. At the bottom, I looked up to see the two staring. My heart was heavy, but I waved as a gesture of reassurance that I was departing with no ill intent. Like that was going to work. Both waved with a look of despondency.

I took a detour and parked the car at Yarran Dheran nature reserve ('Yarran Dheran' is a Wurundjeri term meaning 'wattle gully'). As a child I'd escape to seek refuge here among the clucking wattle birds and cries of the pied currawongs. I wound down the window and sucked in the fresh air and reminisced. I would lay on a bed of wild grass with the odd stone or two pressing against my back, listening to the gurgling of water over rocks. I'd feel the warmth of the sun's rays filtering through the eucalyptus leaves as the trees swayed in rhythm with the southerly breeze. Today the clouds moved low and silent. My eyes tracked the individual branches of a gum, leading to the trunk, and to the base of the tree where the roots lay beneath. Nothing mattered in those moments.

The drive home took longer than usual, my hot head churned with *Where Is My Mind* by the Pixies playing on the radio. I turned up the volume. The timing was apt, a message from God. The traffic moved fast, everyone seemed to be in a hurry along the intersecting highways, desperate to see their partners and kids. I drove slowly, holding back to go nowhere.

I arrived home and sat on the sofa with a heavy heart, consumed by guilt. I played the song again, in my head, "Ooh, stop, ooh, ooh…". Once a song I like has been played on the radio, it remains with me throughout the day and night. I picked up the telephone. "Hi, Mum."
"Ah, Michal."
"How are you, Mum?"
"Not good," she said abruptly.
"I'm sorry, Mum, about what I said today."
"You make me angry."
I anticipated her wrath and the lengthy lecture that followed. I deserved it. I reflected on my visit at Yarran Dheran reserve. My thoughts compared the two states of being: the innocence

of the past, the present damaged man. I wondered what the next chapter would bring.

Marta

I met a girl at a nightclub whose claws dug into me. A tigress named Marta. The nightclub was called Subculture, a hangout for goths and emos in North Melbourne. Marta was tall and nicely shaped with a cracking smile. I introduced myself whilst ordering drinks at the bar. We spoke at length. She took a liking to me. Marta wore a nurse's uniform for Halloween night. The short dress showed off her long legs. She wore a blonde bob tucked behind her ears with a nurse's hat on top.

Jase had given up on the girl who he'd planned to meet. He looked at me with lost eyes, trying to hide his disappointment.

"You comin'?" He said, grabbing his ponytail. "I'm going home."

"Nah, I'm stayin', mate."

He looked up at Marta and back at me. "Ok," he said, "I'll see ya tomorrow." He turned and disappeared into the black.

"My legs are sore," she said. "I need to sit down."

I moved my wheelchair into position. "You can sit on my lap," I replied with a cheeky grin.

"No, I'm too heavy for you!"

"No, you're not."

"Don't lie," she said, sipping from her straw.

I shifted the brake levers to lock the wheels. "Let me show you that you're not."

"No," she said, laughing.

I placed my glass on the floor and held out my arms. Marta turned around and sat gently on my lap.

"Am I too heavy?"

"Not at all. I'll prove it." I wrapped my right forearm under her thighs, the left under her bottom, and lifted her clear off my lap.

She shrieked. "Ok, you can let me down again."

I set her down. "Let's go somewhere private." I handed her my glass. "Hold onto this."

"Woohoo," she yelled, kicking out a leg and holding our drinks aloft as I wheeled away from prying eyes. We made it to the lounge, where couples courted beneath soft lighting. The antique sofa with its red velvet cover set the mood. Marta took off her high heels and rested her legs across my lap. "So, Michael," she said, sipping from her straw. "What do you do for work?"

I picked up my own straw and wrapped it around my finger. "I work for myself. And you? What do you do, Marta?"

"I work for a radio station. I'm an announcer at PBS."

"Oh, cool. I love community radio."

"So," she stared through me, circling the glass edge with her finger. "What happened to you?"

I wrapped the plastic straw tighter till my finger numbed. "Well." I took a deep breath, "I went swimming off Phillip Island. And... well, these seals were swimming nearby off these rocks. So, I swam over and played chasey with them in the swirling water. And, suddenly," I clapped my hands, "A shark attacked me from underneath."

She shrieked with laughter, reminding me of the spotted hyena episode on National Geographic.

She took another sip. "No, what really happened?"

"I had a bad car accident."

She hauled herself up and leaned in close. "How did it happen?"

"I don't wanna talk about it right now." I swallowed a mouthful of vodka and soda.

"Is that from the accident?" she said, stroking the scar on my neck with her fingertips.

"Yes, it's called a tracheostomy."

She placed her drink beside the lamp. Using my shoulders for support, she lifted herself and straddled my crotch. She pulled open the top of my t-shirt and stared down, her hair touching my nose. She smelled of strawberries, sweet and strong.

"What happened here?" she said, pointing to the scar line on my chest.

"You're a nurse, you tell me!"

She laughed and looked at me.

I placed my hands on her hips and moved in. We kissed, and I didn't want to stop.

"Mmmm, you're a cheeky one," she said, placing a finger on my nose. She lifted my shirt and pulled it up, covering my face. "Let's see that scar." My breath blew back onto my face as Marta ran her fingers along the scar, from the top to the base of my chest; her tender touch against the grainy tissue moved me to unfamiliar excitement. She leaned forward and began kissing the tracheostomy scar, circling the fibrous texture with her tongue then nibbling it with warmth. The first thing that came to mind was a chicken McNugget. She continued kissing down the scar line, tickling the pleasure sensors. *Isn't that what the nuggets are made of? Chicken-flavoured tripe?* I cautiously moved my hand down to check the urine bag – it had ballooned to maximum level. I didn't want to go to the toilet for fear of losing the moment, and Marta, altogether. I'd have to make my way through the crowded room, then ask to be lifted up the stairs, and proceed to shimmy my way past the toilet door to piss in a cubicle. I had previously lost out after such tasks, returning to an empty seat or to see her dancing with another. I didn't want to experience that again. I pushed the leg bag behind my calf so Marta wouldn't notice. She stopped kissing, and looked at me. "Was that nice?" she whispered.

"Yes."

"Hmm." She hesitated. "You ok?"

"Yeah."

"I need to pee," she said.

I let out a deep sigh.

"You want another drink on my way back from the loo?"

"A vodka and soda, please," I said, handing her a fifty-dollar note. "And a drink for you too."

Her fingers rummaged through my hair, "Don't move." She stood up and straightened her dress. I watched her walk out of sight. I turned to my left and then right. I twisted the screw open from under my jeans. At first, it was a trickle. I twisted a little more, a steady consistent stream brought on the shame. I pointed the bag away from my shoe, aiming the flow directly under the sofa.

A couple approached. "Hi," I said, pretending to scratch my leg. "How's your night goin'?"

They smiled and continued walking, unaware of my actions. I felt a septic sensation crawl over me like waste bin bugs. I looked down and noticed the damp carpet.

Marta approached, carrying our drinks.

"Hey, look up," I said to her.

She looked up.

I tightened the screw cap, "Don't you think the fake chandeliers look grand?"

"Nyah, they're ok," she said.

The dreaded thought of her repulsion struck me like whiplash.

"Here." She handed me my vodka and soda and resumed her horse-riding position.

"Hey, I have to tell you something."

"Ha, you have a girlfriend?"

"No."

"Then tell me," she said, stroking my hair with a cigarette in hand.

Nausea crept in. "In the accident, my urethra got torn up. That's the tissue between my bladder and penis, which means I can't piss like I used to."

She took a draw from her cigarette and blew out a steady stream of smoke, looking at me with sedated eyes. "So, how do you pee?"

I cleared my throat, "I have a catheter that empties the urine from my bladder."

"Nawww," she said with careless apathy.

I had anticipated a reaction of horror.

"So, we're all fucked up in some way or another," she said, lifting her straw from the glass. "Where's this catheter thing of yours?"

"Underneath my shirt. There's a stoma, or a hole, in my bladder." I lifted the glass, took a mouthful of drink and swallowed hard.

"Can I see it?"

I was surprised by her apparent casualness. She looked at me in readiness. I unbuttoned my jeans to reveal the repulsive set-up. *Please, don't think about kissing it.*

"Oh wow, cool," she said, touching the edge.

"No, don't touch!"

She withdrew her fingers.

"Sorry, it's just… meant to be sterile."

She leaned forward and kissed my neck, then moved onto my mouth. She slipped her hands under my shirt, pressing her fingernails into the skin. "Can we go now?" she whispered in my ear. The terror ran deep as I contemplated all that could go wrong into the night.

I pushed the thoughts away, acting calm. "Yep, let's get out of here." I wheeled past the witches and vampires, with Marta leading the way. We arrived at the passenger door of a waiting taxi. The driver insisted on dismantling the chair, dropping the wheels with a clattering sound. He turned and twisted the chair, fumbling to fold it. I buried my face in my hands.

Marta held my arm in support. "Don't fret," she laughed, "it's ok."

"Here, let me do it, mate." I folded the chair from the edge of the back seat.

The driver placed the chair in the boot and slammed it closed once, twice, and a third time.

We arrived at my place.

"I'm busting to pee. Where's the toilet?"

"Down the corridor, and on to your right."

I fought off self-doubt as I set wine and glasses on the table and lowered the lighting. I turned on the stereo and played Nirvana *Unplugged*. Hearing the toilet flush heightened my nerves.

She entered the dining room, adjusting the hem of her dress. "Oh, wine!" She sat down next to me, helping herself to a glass. She opened her handbag and produced a sleek tube with what appeared to be a pre-rolled joint. "You don't mind if we smoke weed?"

I lost the power to say no. "Yeah… nah it's cool."

She tweaked the end of the roll.

"I haven't smoked for a long time," I said, hoping for sympathy in my attempts.

My last experience of smoking a joint in company terrified me. My bones felt like they were attached by cotton threads, much like a puppet. I kept looking up to see who held the strings.

I watched as Marta lit up the joint, admiring her smoking technique. She passed the joint to me between delicate fingers. I inhaled small amounts when she wasn't watching, only to inhale deeper when she was. The distinct, pungent taste rested on my tongue as the relaxation opened a magical portal. I placed the joint on the porcelain saucer, the ashtray for the night. "I need to tell you something."

"You're married?"

"No," I laughed.

"You know how I told you I had an accident?"

She sat up, perched on my pancake legs. "Yeah?"

"Well, it happened on duty. I'm a policeman." I again anticipated a negative reaction.

"Oh?"

"Yeah. I don't want you to think less of me."

She laughed. "I'm smoking weed in front of a cop."

"Nah, I don't give a shit about that."

"Were you on a police chase?"

"No, going to a 'shots fired' call out. Like, 'Heidelberg Unit, we have shots fired at such-and-such address'," I said, mimicking the radio operator. I looked into her eyes. "It's too long a story to talk about it, for now." I looked down at her soft mouth, back to her eyes again, and smiled. I leaned in and kissed her, holding her chin softly to savour the moment. I moved my hand over her legs and slipped it between them, pressing firmly on her inner thighs.

Marta pulled away and looked at me, "You're cheeky, Mr Policeman."

I leaned in and kissed her again, making my way along her neck.

Marta pushed me away and stood up, lifted the hem of her dress and straddled me. Leaning in, she caressed the skin of my neck with her lips, soft and warm. She lifted and removed my shirt and proceeded to unbutton my jeans. I placed my hand to stop her from going further. "Um… the catheter."

"Hey," she pushed away my hand. She continued to unzip my pants. The catheter stuck out like a weed.

I was afraid that she'd be disgusted seeing the tube from the stoma to the leg bag.

Marta tried to pull the tight jeans below my waist.

I held up my hand. "Wait."

She placed a finger against my lips, "Shh." She stood up, unzipped her white uniform, and wiggled her bottom to allow the dress to fall at her feet, revealing red lingerie. I couldn't believe such a Scandinavian-looking stunner would have an interest in me. *She should be with someone more deserving.* The drilling voice went on, *I'm unworthy of her.*

She turned in slow circles with her arms behind her head, dancing to the music; her hands gliding down the sides of her hips. She removed her bra; Botticelli's *Birth of Venus* came to mind. Her naked figure stood before me in all its beauty.

My mind played tricks on me – Mum and Dad appeared in the background; Mum watching with curiosity and Dad looking particularly pleased. I dug my thumbnails into my index fingers, trying to focus my attention on Marta.

She walked over and straddled my legs, her small breasts staring at me. I turned her palms upward and kissed them; I continued kissing up her arm, then onto her slender neck, and finally to her soft lips. She grabbed my crotch. Blood rushed to my head, matching the beating heart of dread. I feared my lack of manhood would turn her off.

I removed her hand. "It doesn't work," I whispered.

"Hey?" She persisted, trying to reach in and rub my penis.

I forced her hand off. "It… doesn't work." The long silence made the situation more painful.

"Why can't you?" She looked at me, waiting for a quick answer.

"Coz of the accident."

"You can do it," she said, placing her hands around my face as though pleading.

I'd heard those words before.

"We can make it work."

"Don't worry, just concentrate."

The words carried good intentions to reassure and encourage. In truth, they took the shape of daggers, piercing my rib cage and tearing into the flesh.

I resisted the temptation, like many times before, to inject my penis with chemicals. The needle would bend as I pushed through the seal in haste to withdraw the liquid and insert the chemical-filled needle into the phallus, causing my penis to balloon black and blue; all the while, she'd wait, wondering what

I was doing in the bathroom. I pitied my penis for undergoing such brutality, asking him for forgiveness.

"It doesn't work coz of the accident."

She held both of my hands, "You can do it." She slowly let go and slid down onto her back with the rug beneath her, waiting for my approach. I removed my shoes, socks and jeans; only the cotton boxer shorts remained, exposing my matchstick legs. Her hands grasped my hair, moving away from my failed construct, much to my relief. The catheter lining twisted and pulled on the bladder as I moved into position. And, like the famous Italian castrati without a prelude to serenade, my fingers did the singing. I wanted to prove to her I was an excellent lover to make up for my lack of manhood. Marta closed her eyes; her body moved in rhythm. The sweet smell of sex intensified, her moans melding with the vocals of Kurt Cobain in the background. Her head turned to the side, revealing vulnerability, the elongated muscle from ear to collarbone defined by excitement.

"You're beautiful," I whispered close to her ear.

The late morning sun roused my stiffened body, my head banging like a jackhammer. My blurred eyes watched over her pretty face. Lying next to her was pure gold. She awoke to find me staring at her.

"Look at your bed hair!" She giggled, ruffling my thick mane.

"It's a good look, don't you think?"

She laughed.

I uncoiled the tube from around my leg. I looked down to see rusty-coloured urine; infection was sure to follow. But I didn't care, the pay-off was worth it.

Marta sat up facing me with the bedsheet up to her shoulders, staring at the scar line. "How long were you in the hospital for?"

"Seven months."

She reached forward, tracing the scar line down my chest with her fingertip. "Oh wow," she followed the scar curving around the torso, its shape as a scythe. "Were you in much pain?"

"Some days were good, some were bad." I turned and looked her in the eye. "It was more painful in my head than my body." I chuckled. "I put away criminals for a living, yet I get rewarded by being caged in a hospital, my private hell."

She leaned in, smiled with kindness, and kissed me softly.

The front door latch opened. "Michal?" Dad called out. I had forgotten he kept a spare key to the house. I looked at Marta with dread.

He plodded through the lounge room. "Michal, I have some mortadella and bocconcini."

"Who's that?" she whispered.

"That's Dad," I said, shaking my head, a rush of blood filling my cheeks.

"Does he live with you?"

"No." I paused. "He drops in without warning to drop off groceries. He buys them in bulk coz they're on special. He does it as a favour… but it annoys me."

Marta shrieked with laughter. I clutched my hair with both hands. I heard the bags land on the kitchen table and the fridge door open and close.

"I leave dem in de fridge, Michal."

I thought of the lingering smell of last night's party. "Our clothes are all over the floor," I said quietly.

She laughed out loud.

I buried my head beneath the sheets.
"I'm going now. Bye, Michal."

She bit down on her lower lip, staring at me with her soft blue eyes. "Have you got a spare jumper for me?"

I loaned her my winter jumper, a rag cotton favourite. She sat on the back patio with her knees tucked under the jumper and lit a cigarette.

I called out from the kitchen window, "Would you like some tea or orange juice?"

"I'll have coffee, thanks."

"Ah, I don't have coffee, sorry."

"Tea is fine."

I placed the cup between my thighs and wheeled the chair over to her, spilling tea over the sides and onto my jeans.

"Do you need help?"

"Nah, I can manage."

I knew better than to handle a hot mug of tea between my legs. I positioned my chair next to her, without a top, posing my upper torso for her eyes to feast on.

She looked up. "I need to go home," she said.

I swallowed a mouthful of tea, burning my throat. "Ok." I wasn't prepared for her to make her exit so quickly. The voice inside reminded me I was a mere subject of Her Majesty.

"Can I ask you something?" she said, blowing a steady stream of smoke.

I scratched my arm. "Yeah."

"Why don't you have a girlfriend?"

The question I'd been asked many times before. "I do."

She looked surprised by my answer.

"It depends on the day of the week…"

She shrieked with laughter. "No, seriously?"

I pressed my thumbnail into the opposite hand, scratching it back and forth. I inhaled deeply through my nose and exhaled, "I don't know." I leaned forward with elbows on my knees, staring through the dark gap between the deck panels. I lit up a cigarette, sat up straight and stretched out my arms. "Where do you live?"

"Altona," she said, exhaling a stream of smoke.

"Do you need a lift?" I felt obliged to drive her.

"No, I'll catch a cab. Thank you anyway." She peeled away. "Can I use your phone to call one?" she said, forcing a smile with raised eyebrows.

I felt vulnerable, and I didn't want to show it. "Yeah, sure," I said, leaning against the post. I didn't want her to go.

She returned with folded arms, snug in my jumper. "It's on its way."

"Hey, can I call you sometime?" I blurted.

She grabbed my hand. "I enjoyed last night." Her look had me prepared for the predictable. "I have to tell you… I'm engaged."

The sting of her words burned inside me. "Oh… how long have you been engaged?"

"A year."

"So, where is this guy of yours?"

"He's flying somewhere over the Pacific right now. He's a pilot."

I felt small in comparison to the intrepid aviator.

"We're taking a break… kinda," she said, before pursing her lips.

The taxi driver sounded his horn in the driveway. She handed me a sheet of lined paper from my notepad.

"Here, call me." Her number was inscribed with a love heart. "Can I keep this?" She asked, referring to the jumper. "I'll give it back when I see you next."

"Yeah, sure."

She kissed me on the cheek. "Bye, Mr Policeman."

Later that evening, the intermittent nerve pain came in wave-like motions with sudden burning sharpness into my lower back and both legs. *Welcome back, friend.* The pain was consistent with previous urinary tract infections. I learnt quickly to sing a chosen song in my head to drown out the pain's chorus. But the one with pitchfork was too strong.

We continued seeing each other. Marta surprised me; she'd take off my sunglasses unexpectedly and say, "I want to see your eyes." On her radio shifts, she'd send out, "A big cheerio to Michael," or say, "This one goes out to you, Michael Tarulli." She'd move in sync with the beat on the dance floor, while rival guys tried their luck to lure her; she'd smile to put me at ease, but my sitting bones would ache with the thought of her slipping away.

I called daily. "What colour knickers are you wearing today?"

She would cackle, and I'd pull the phone away from my ear.

I lay on the sofa thinking of Marta. There was something different about her that was more than a feeling, more than lust. She ignited a passion in me; a belief in the possibility of a relationship with her. There was also a feeling that suggested it was not a good idea to pursue her, but I fought against this.

I organised a romantic picnic at the botanical gardens in the city. The two of us enjoyed cheese and champagne. Her head rested on my legs, looking up at me lovingly. As she spoke, the familiar pain commenced in my intestines. I wasn't sure whether I was gassy or not. *Can I fart in her presence or hold off?*

After a few minutes passed, I realised that it wasn't gas, so I spoke to my guts, *Don't you dare make your move now.* The pain came in waves. I tried diplomacy, *Just hold on a little longer, ok?* I stared at Marta with alarm. *Just a little longer, please, for me?*

Marta took off her sunglasses, "What's up?"

The dark shadow amused himself, whispering the words, "Arise, oh anxious one." *I can never get an even break.*

"You'll have to excuse me," I said, lifting her head off my thighs. I crawled onto the wheelchair and worked away at the wheels toward the toilet block. "God, help me," I mumbled. "Yep, right now would be good, big fella." I entered the urine-saturated cell, adjusting my vision to darkness as the overhead light failed to operate. I made out the shape of the porcelain bowl and went to work on dropping my trousers. It was too late. "Why the fuck would you do this to me?" I said aloud. The sweat dripped down my chest as I assessed the spoiled underwear. I wrapped the smelly garment with toilet paper to the size of a soccer ball so the cleaner needn't notice it, and threw it in the bin. I was conscious of Marta, *will she suspect that I had an accident?* I pumped out liquid soap from the dispenser and washed the spoiled area of my jeans, rinsed and dried them under the hot air blower. *Please, don't come down to check on me.* I brought them up to my nose. *They still smell.*

When I arrived back, Marta's facial expression told me she suspected the obvious but she didn't let on otherwise.

"Are you ok?" she said, sipping her champagne.

"Umm," I rubbed my hands against the jeans, "Can we go home?"

She called on the phone. "When can I see you? We need to talk." These words crept into my veins like a weed.

I had a feeling this wasn't going to turn out well, it suffocated my patience. After four months, my hope for more than a trivial dalliance with Marta began to wane.

I drove my Falcon to the city to meet her at the Hard Rock Café on the corner of Spring and Bourke streets. I sat opposite her at the dining table, hardly touching my meal. The mood was different – distant and distorted.

"We shouldn't see each other," she said.

The words cut me deep as I went into a state of numbness. The nagging voice in my head reverberated with the "you're unworthy" chant.

"Why?"

"I need time alone. I need to find myself again…"

I disguised the pain with a calm performance, listening to her confession as though I was a counsellor. I warmed to the idea of performing a Harry Houdini act, to disappear. But I was not that person; I was a sucker for punishment, preferring to sit it out.

After our meal, we walked to my car in the misty rain. Marta reached out to hold my hand; I obliged, it lacked warmth. We sat in my car, parked outside Parliament House. The light rain on the windscreen slightly obscured our view of the majestic Windsor Hotel.

"Are you ok?" she said, breaking the silence.

I nodded without looking at her. I stared, marvelling at the colours: the red tail-lights of passing cars, the orange, yellow and green street lights, all combined into a mosaic-like sparkle, then pooled to form teardrops, only to run down the glass.

She placed her hand under my chin, guiding me to meet her eyes. "We'll be friends, yeah?"

"Yeah." *I'd rather perform* seppuku, *the act of disembowelment, than remain friends.*

"Are you sure you're ok?"

"Yeah," I said, pressing my lips to force a smile.

She moved forward and gave me a final goodbye kiss on the lips.

I occasionally found blonde hair strands on my pillow. The smell of her on my jumper, too, was cruel. I missed her quirky laugh, her smiling face, the taste of her lips. I tried to forget her, carrying on with my nightly exploits, escorting the ladies on my lap. But no one came close to matching the likes of Marta. *If only I tried harder to keep her, to convince her I was worthwhile.* But I couldn't force this on her. I wanted Marta to choose me of her own free will. Like holding a ladybird in hand, keeping her from dancing in the wind would've been unfair.

Three months after I farewelled Marta, I crossed paths with her again. She was walking hand-in-hand with a policeman I knew in Swan Street, Richmond. Darren, also known as Dazza, was the alpha male – a jock type, tall with broad shoulders. It was an awkward encounter; I offered a courtesy greeting of "Hello, how are you?" to save face before parting.

The encounter with Marta and her new beau stayed with me long into the days and nights after. Runaway thoughts, as if I was watching my life in a movie, chased through my mind. I questioned how I appeared to women; I thought about my encounters; I wondered if I was cheap entertainment for them; I considered if it was out of sympathy that they made an effort to please me. I concluded it was a combination of all of the above.

The burning desire was persistent. I wanted more. I wanted to feel desired, to be loved and no less of a person than my peers. However, I feared fate would not allow it. I felt my family and friends were getting on with their lives, leaving me behind. I was searching for reason amid the drinking and womanising, and the plagued thought that nothing was going right for me kept repeating. I felt there was no one I could talk to, confide in, or seek support from.

I'd go to sleep by imagining myself curled up in the middle of a lotus flower, resting over a body of water, its petals protecting me from the outside noise. Even in the quietest moments, the echoes whispered. *What if I write Marta a letter to win back her heart? Will I dare say I love her? Will my intentions offend her, or will I make a fool of myself?*

A Pretender

My stomach gurgled as I pushed my wheelchair to the train station. It was going to be a forty-five-minute train ride to the city so I purchased a salami sandwich at the Box Hill station food court. Resting at a table, I separated the slices of bread to see how thick the salami was. I was disappointed. They didn't make them the way Dad used to when I was a kid, with meat slices about half an inch thick between large, crusty pieces of bread. As I commenced eating, I recognised a familiar face in the distance – it was Kath Daly, my women's studies lecturer from the humanities course I did at TAFE.

Kath had spent hours outside class helping me with language I didn't understand from authors like Germaine Greer and Simone de Beauvoir. I trusted and admired her, and after some time felt safe letting down my guard down with her. I confessed that I lacked confidence with my studies, and said how difficult I was finding essay writing. She encouraged me to continue learning. I confided in her about a girl I liked, who I couldn't ask out on a date for fear of rejection. She smiled and said, "What's the worst that could happen if she did say no?"

Thinking about it now, I'm sure she saw a naïve young man trying to overcome his fears.

I took a deep breath and wheeled over to her, smiling nervously. "Hi, Kath."

"Hello," she said looking surprised. "And how do I know you?"

I smiled. "C'mon, you know who I am."

"No… you'll have to help me out." She placed a finger on her lips. "You're a past student?"

"The only guy in women's studies." I laughed.

"Oh, Michael! Yes, of course." She looked at my wheelchair, puzzled and shocked. "What happened, if you don't mind me asking?"

I told her the story of my accident.

"Oh, Michael." She placed her hand on her chest. Her eyes scanned me from head to toe. I must've looked a pitiful sight. "Are they looking after you?"

I shrugged my shoulders, "Yeah, kind of."

Kath placed a hand over her mouth, shaking her head. "Michael, I would never have thought of you as a policeman." Her eyes were soft and sympathetic. "It's not you."

I felt the heat rise to my face. "I've always wanted to be a policeman, Kath." I smiled; my cheeks cramped with the discomfort.

"No." She shook her head slowly. "It's the wrong job for you."

The spear pierced my armour.

"It's not who you are."

I took in a deep breath. "Kath, I'm okay." I leaned back, my hands steadying the chair.

She looked at me as if doubting my words.

"Really, I'm doin' okay."

"What have they got you doing?"

"I'm working in the city, as a criminal analyst." My confidence came to the fore as I continued. "I'm given information from field officers about a series of crimes. I research them, studying patterns and trends in an attempt to identify the suspect." I looked at Kath for her approval.

"Sounds interesting. Do you enjoy it?"

"Yeah, I do." I folded my arms. "I've yet to be qualified as an analyst but I'm working on that. So, what are you up to these days?"

"I'm lecturing at La Trobe University."

"Are you enjoying it?"

"Yes, I am." She rolled her eyes. "The workload is overwhelming as usual."

"I can imagine… well, great to see you, Kath." I pointed my thumb in the direction of my table. "Gotta get back to my sandwich before the cleaner gets rid of it."

She offered a motherly smile. "Look after yourself, Michael."

"I will," I said, trying to remain upbeat. "See ya." I waved and pushed my chair toward my table. I looked back to see Kath staring and waving at me in a way that reminded me of Mum when she dropped me off at prep as a five-year-old.

Back at my table, I ate the tasteless sandwich with Kath's words vibrating in my mind. They continued to haunt me through the train journey and into my working hours until, four hours later, it was time to leave. "I'm going home now, guys."

"What?" Nash said with a sarcastic laugh. "You just got here!"

"Yep, and I'm going now, to see my boyfriend."

Wayne erupted in laughter.

I sat on the sofa that night watching a comedy skit on TV. The punchlines went over my head – I was distracted by Kath's words, "It's not who you are." The truth pounded away in my grey matter, reminding me I was a pretender, a fake. I had chosen the wrong path. At night, before I closed my eyes, I'd lay on my bed hugging the pillow, dreaming of gentle hands, lots of them, comforting me like fallen flower petals; time and again I'd wake up in a sweat with my arms flailing. The nocturnal terrors I had had since the accident – from punching into DJ's face to grabbing the collars of faceless men in uniform and yelling obscenities at them – continued unabated.

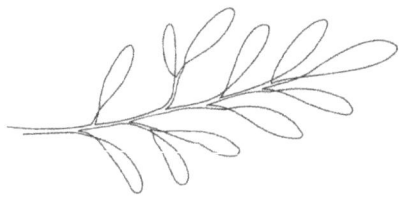

Paesano

I was unaware I had been assigned to a rehabilitation officer until a year since I returned to work on modified duties, when I received a call from Tony de De Romeis. He was older than me and carried a heavy Italian accent. He introduced himself as a *paesano* (a compatriot of Italian descent), indicating a shared familiarity and identification between second-generation Italians. Tony had been brought up in the northern suburbs where there was a dense population of Italian migrants. I felt at ease with him as he continued to tell me of his background. We shared similar upbringings: when in trouble, our fathers would chase us around the dining table attempting to beat us with a leather belt; failing to do so, they would throw a shoe at us. We also shared a reluctance to play soccer, preferring Aussie rules – much to our fathers' disappointment.

Tony requested to meet and discuss my current return to work program.

The next day Tony arrived with his sleeves rolled up and a loosened necktie. "How's it going Cheech?" he called out.

"Enjoying the work?"

"Yeah, all good," I said with a tired smile.

"Are you sure, Cheech?"

I didn't answer.

"Come," he said with a flick of his head. "Follow me."

We took up our discussion in one of the available interview rooms. He closed the door and sat down opposite me. "You know what the wogs say in the old country? *'Quando un amico chiede, non v'è domani'* (When a friend asks, there's no tomorrow)."

I laughed, it was like being with Nonno Joe again.

"So, tell me, what's on your mind?"

I let out a sigh, "I don't like it here."

"Okay, can you tell me why?"

I shrugged my shoulders, "Just don't like it here." I pressed my thumbnail into the palm of my hand.

"Okay," he scratched his head. "We can find work elsewhere if you like?"

I nodded my head.

"No problem. Let me do some homework. Ok, Cheech?"

I nodded again. "Thanks."

A position was available at the Youth Advisory Unit, considered by many as a "feel-good" job for its approach to juvenile crime and prevention initiatives. The unit worked in cooperation with the Children's Court of Victoria and youth justice workers. Tony had arranged for my transfer to the unit. He accompanied me on my last shift at Transit Patrol. I looked at Wayne, who smiled, trying hard not to let his sadness show.

"See ya," he said.

I smiled back. "See ya, mate." I wheeled away with slow pushes. Tony led the way out of the office.

I stopped and turned around. "Hey, Nash!" I threw my bracelet at him. "Something to remember me by."

Man-Mountain Andy

It was September 1995 when I joined the Youth Advisory Unit. On my first day I was introduced to Chief Inspector Rod Norman.

He shook my hand, "Welcome aboard."

He was the highest-ranking officer I had ever worked with, and he resembled a teddy bear. I learned he was a former detective of the Major Crime Squad. I was also introduced to Maureen, the secretary.

"Pleased to meet you," she said with a timid voice. I liked her immediately.

Rod led me to a partition with a desk and a computer. "Here is your work area," he said tapping his fingers on the edge of the panel. "You'll be given a portfolio to work through at your own pace.

"Thanks, boss."

"Oh yeah, I forgot," he said, stopping abruptly before turning back to me. "You'll be working with Andy Walsh from Juvenile Justice – you can't miss him," he said with a chuckle.

Standing with a folder under his arm, watching me push the wheelchair toward him, was a mountain of a man. I estimated him to be two metres tall; his shoulders were as wide as goalposts. I noticed him chewing gum.

"Andy Walsh," he said, extending his hand to shake mine. "Pleased to meet ya."

I stopped. "Hi, Michael Tarulli, nice to meet you." His handshake almost broke my metacarpals.

"I'm from Juvenile Justice," he said. "We'll be working together." He continued chewing his gum. "Is this your desk?" He pointed to my cubicle.

"Yes." I moved the wheelchair as close as I could so that my knees cleared the desktop.

He sat down opposite me and propped his elbows on his knees. "So, tell me, how are ya?"

I was surprised by his forthright approach. "Oh, I'm doing all right."

"You had a bad car accident, I hear?"

"Yeah, a few years ago now."

He shook his head. "Shhhit. How many operations have you had?"

"I've had a few."

His forehead creased in the middle and his eyes narrowed. I could tell he wanted to know more. He seemed genuinely empathetic, so I summoned the energy to continue. "I've had operations on my chest, abdomen and pelvis. Almost died."

He sat up and folded his arms. "Jesus."

"Well, not quite."

He maintained his shocked look without registering the joke, chewing slowly on his gum. "If you don't mind me asking, are you in much pain?"

"Not at the moment," I said, scratching at my palm. "At times it sneaks up on me though."

He shook his head and looked me in the eye. "You're a brave fella. Anything you need, anything, just give me a yell."

"Thanks."

I knew we'd get along. The intuitive feeling that came alive after our introduction was confirmed in the months that followed.

One day, Andy introduced me to his friend over a coffee catch-up in Fitzroy. His name was Michael Maloney. He spoke with an accent like those at 10 Downing Street, and was distinguishable by his whimsical bow tie and multicoloured shirt, all of which impressed me. At my first consultation with Michael, I thought he was just another annoying psychiatrist. I'd seen several before him.

His first words were, "So, tell me from the start. How did the accident occur?"

Anger crept into the fissures of my brain. "Do we have to go through this again?"

"Yes, we're going to whether you like it or not," he replied sharply, giving a "don't mess with me" stare.

From that moment, Michael became a cornerstone of my existence. Listening to his words of truth opened my eyes to see the strength that lay within. He knew me better than I knew myself. In his presence, I poured out my heart, cried uncontrollably, and laughed aloud.

At work, I found the administrative work challenging, and at times tedious. My research was to validate the department's plan for deterrence-oriented programs for juvenile delinquency. I'd often look over my shoulder to find my supervisor, Sergeant Van Beek, standing there watching me. He was second in charge to Rod Norman. He reminded me of the graffiti icon Foo Was Here, always checking over my shoulder when I was typing out reports or researching material on the internet.

With a poker face, he'd say, "Michael, this report is missing key data elements." He might as well have said it was shit.

I entered a report writing course with the police skills and training department. I became familiar with big words and concepts like stakeholders, recidivism, strategic planning, longitudinal studies and implementation. The experience of learning new skills empowered me; I foolishly believed I was capable of leapfrogging my peers to seniority. I also wanted to impress Rod Norman by showing that I had the intelligence to use the language of declassified CIA documents that you see on TV. Still, I struggled with the changes imposed on me. I'd write reports over and over, making sure they were at least presentable.

Every day, I pushed my chair along the concourse that separated the two buildings of the Victoria Police Centre. Building A housed crime squads, the training centre where I attended writing class, and the offices of high-ranking Commissioners. Building B accommodated specialist units such as the Youth Advisory Unit and Aboriginal Affairs. On this occasion I was headed to deliver reports to my instructor at the training centre, when I noticed an officer walking toward me. His lapels distinguished him as an Assistant Commissioner. I maintained a steady pace, avoiding eye contact.

"Mr Tarully," the officer called out.

I stopped and sat straight with my chest out. "Sir."

He leant forward, extending his hand to shake mine. "Graham Sinclair."

I made sure my grip matched his handshake. *Another bone breaker.*

"It's a pleasure to meet you, Michael."

"Thank you, Sir."

"You're working under Rod Norman at the Youth Advisory Unit, I understand?"

"Yes, I am, Sir." I maintained a steady smile.

"You can call me Graham," he said with a calm voice. "How are you finding the work?"

"It's great, Sir," I paused, scrambling for words to fill the gaps. "I'm finding the work interesting. I believe I can make a difference there."

"That's great to hear. I assume you have career aspirations?"

The question caught me off guard. "I'm thinking of doing a uni course to supplement my promotion, Sir," I lied. I wasn't sure what I was doing at the present moment let alone in the future.

"Ok," he said, looking surprised. "What interests you?"

"Industrial relations." It was the first thing that came to mind.

His eyes widened and he leaned back. "You'll need all the help you can get dealing with the unions," he said with a chuckle.

The heat surfaced to my cheeks.

"Well, great to have you with us again, young man."

The unexpected reception from the Assistant Commissioner warmed me. I continued on my way with renewed energy.

I was preparing a report for the upcoming meeting of the District Commanders Youth Forum when the pain hit me. I leant forward, resting my head on the keyboard, thumping my fist on the desk. The devil with his pitchfork struck my right leg at ten second intervals. My left leg would be struck with shots of fire immediately after. I grabbed my shinbones. "Piss off, will ya?" I lifted my left trouserleg and noticed dark-coloured urine with blobs of sediment resting on the bottom. *Yep, again.* These were signs of a blocked catheter and likely infection. The catheter needed changing.

Maureen stood up from behind her desk. "Are you right, Michael?" She took off her glasses.

"Oh Maurs, sorry." I looked down at my feet. "Just some pain." My pelvic bones screamed. I slid off my wheelchair and lay on the floor. *If only I could detach myself like Lego blocks.*

Andy approached with a folder in hand, chewing gum. "You right, Mick?"

I looked up at the colossus. "Mate, I'm struggling a bit."

"Jesus." The wrinkles on his forehead deepened. "Stay there."

I'm not going anywhere in a hurry.

"I'll get ya some water. Do you need a pillow?"

I nodded my head. Staring at the ceiling I noticed the white quartered panels had coffee-coloured stains. *Oh, look, a map of Tassie.*

Andy returned and placed a pillow under my head. "There you go, mate. Stay there."

Maureen followed with a folded blanket. "Here, Michael," she said, draping the blanket over me. She reminded me of Florence Nightingale.

The smell of latex from the pillow was a sickly reminder of my time imprisoned at the Austin hospital.

"Young Tarulli, the man of notoriously vicious and intemperate disposition," Rod quipped, standing aside with hands on hips. I laughed with effort. The line was a shared joke between us. It was was taken from the movie *Unforgiven*, and I'd say it when enraged or shitty.

"How bad is the pain?"

"Comes and goes boss, but I'm ok."

Maureen shook her head.

"We can arrange for medical assistance if you need it?"

"Nah, boss, I've got medication for it. I'm used to it." I rummaged through my carry bag for the prescribed drugs.

"Rest for now," Rod said calmly. "When you're ready, let me know. I'll get one of the boys to drive you home."

Once home, my anxiety increased with the thought of changing the catheter. "Please work with me," I said, opening the medical dressing pack. I took a few breaths as I leaned back into the chair and pressed firmly with my left fingers around the base of the catheter. I took a breath in, and on the exhale tugged at the brown silicon tube. It failed to withdraw. Sweat beads ran down the sides of my torso. "Ok, let's do this again." I twisted the catheter and yanked it at left and right angles. It failed to give way. I looked at the stoma with calmness. "We're gonna do this." I relaxed my abdominal muscles and took a few deep breaths. On the second exhale I firmly pulled the catheter. Much to my relief, the silicon tube slid out with ease. Warm urine flowed over my abdomen and sides. I quickly inserted the new tube and emptied the remaining waste into the toilet.

The following year, 1996, I spent so much time seated at my work desk that an ulcer developed over my coccyx. I had increased my working hours, from six to eight a day. Sitting long hours meant that the protruding coccyx was pressing against the chair. I could not feel the irritation or the problem it was causing. I ran my fingers over the sacral area after showering one day and felt fluid moving around under the skin. Rarely did I want to see the disfigurement of my frail image in the mirror, for it repulsed me, but on this occasion I had to. Lying down to see better, I noticed a swollen sac had grown over the sacrum and was on the verge of bursting. If left unchecked the condition would lead to sepsis and bone infection. The consulting surgeon recommended the removal of bone from the coccyx and sacrum. I became a patient in a hospital again, this time at Cabrini Private in Malvern. I lay on my side for weeks until the wound healed.

Once the skin healed over the sacral area I could return to work. I was approached by Andy not long after. He had read an article in the newspaper about a physiotherapist, Gavin Williams, who was working with spinal patients and amputees at the Epworth Rehabilitation Centre in Richmond, helping them to regain the ability to walk after road trauma.

"Have a read of this Mick," he said, chewing gum. "This bloke can help ya walk again." Andy by this stage knew of the slight kicking ability of my right leg. He had noticed this when we sat for coffee at the cafeteria and meetings in the conference room. The first time he observed it he asked, "Can you move your legs?"

"Yeah, the right one I can… a little." I looked down at my atrophied leg and demonstrated a weak kicking action. "I used to kick the footy with my right."

I read the article, which included a photo of Gavin. I recognised him. I had been introduced to Gavin through a friend at an athletics club, a few years before my accident. He wore the same distinct broad smile. I remembered his friendly demeanour.

Andy gave me the nudge I needed to reignite my determination to walk again. There was something holding me back. It took me a while to overcome the guilt wearing on my mind for those who I knew would never walk again. I felt that if I was to walk again I'd betray the likes of Shannon and Big Jim.

I recalled the secret pact I had made with my friend the gum tree – from my hospital bed, I had sworn to the tree outside my window that I would walk again.

Andy looked me in the eye. "You'll walk again Mick."

The Quest to Walk

My first consultation with Gavin proved a turning point in my quest to walk. I demonstrated my ability to move the right lower leg in a kicking action whilst sitting. The movement was enough to kick a golf ball into a putting hole from about a metre away. He asked if I could move my left leg.

"Stand back," I said jokingly.

Gavin placed his hand above the knee joint. "Kick out your leg."

I grimaced. "I'm trying." I could feel a muscle twitch but the movement was ever-so-slight.

He stood up and scratched his chin with a studied look. "I reckon we can strengthen both legs."

I was taken aback by his casualness, like it was no big deal. Hearing his words sparked the fire within me.

I knew the journey wasn't going to be easy. From once to twice a week I attended the Epworth Rehabilitation Centre in Richmond. I toiled away, moving my matchstick legs against every slight resistance. I squeezed an inflated ball between my thighs. I laid on my side and kicked my legs along the vinyl table with a non-abrasive cloth underneath to avoid friction.

"I remember my legs back in school, shaped like an Olympian's." I looked Gavin in the eye. "Damn they looked sexy," I chuckled.

"Carl Lewis, hey?" Gavin said with his bare-all-teeth smile.

"Ah, not quite."

About six months into my rehabilitation my left knee had become so rigid that it failed to straighten. Gavin placed a ten-kilogram plate flat onto my knee to straighten it. He placed a sandbag on top of the weight and left it sitting there for ten minutes.

"How's that feel?" he asked.

"Bloody hell… you know how to torture."

He laughed. "No pain, no gain. Isn't that what bodybuilders say?"

"You're enjoying this aren't you?"

This procedure progressed from ten to fifteen minutes, and to twenty over time. Satisfied the knee had straightened to his content, Gavin constructed a plaster mould on my left leg. The cast was cut sideways, the two equal lengths acting as a splint. Cotton webbing was used to strap the cast to my leg. I slept with the splint overnight to maintain the straightened form. Many nights the pain struck like a thunderbolt down my leg, interrupting my sleep. I kept playing ACDC's "Thunderstruck" in my head to distract myself from the pain. It worked, sometimes.

I intensified my strengthening and cardio program, pacing back and forth with the support of parallel bars. When my left leg got tired, Gavin stood behind ready to catch my fall. I'd stare and rub my left quadricep muscles when resting. *Catch up with your brother, will ya?* Winter or summer, it didn't matter, the heat in the room was unforgiving – the sweat ran down the centre of my chest as my legs began to buckle. A chair was brought to my aid.

"Good work, Mike."

The Ultimate Challenge

I received a telephone call from a journalist wishing to interview me for an article to appear in *Australian Safety News*, a union publication. I looked around for prying eyes.

"Um, why interview me?"

"We're interviewing injured workers and your name came up. Your story will attract a lot of interested readers."

"Ok." I was excited at the thought of being famed in a magazine for my tale of survival. I downplayed my feelings to the interviewer.

"It will feature in our October issue (1996), coinciding with Health and Safety Week. Would you be interested?"

"Umm, yeah, why not."

With Rod Norman's permission, the interview took place at the Youth Advisory Unit. The interviewer asked me about the work I performed there.

"I'm helping to design youth diversionary programs to keep young people out of Juvenile Justice centres. For one, I'm working with the Children's Court and Department of Human

Services in constructing a framework called 'family group conferencing'. It allows the young offender and victim of the crime to convene in the presence of family members of both parties, the police officer who laid the charges, and a mediator. A resolution is agreed between the parties on what needs to be done about the harm caused by the offence. An outcome plan is prepared that sets out the agreements that were made."

Then came the hard questions regarding the accident and my injuries.

A copy of *Australian Safety News* landed on my desk in a sealed envelope about a month later. The interview was titled "The Angry Man", which I was deeply embarrassed by. The publication covered two pages. I looked around to see if anyone was within distance of my cubicle. I read my responses to the interviewer's questions, most notably, "I find my situation very frustrating, and I have not accepted it. I get angry, I get angry with the doctors, I get angry with the driver. I get angry with myself."

I paused, surprised at how upfront I had been, a confession of my state of mind. I planted my face in the palm of my hands and massaged my eyeballs. I tossed the magazine aside and resumed typing my reports with a surge of satisfaction rising from the pit of my gut.

Another interview took place, this time with *Police Life*, in June 1997. I opened up the magazine and saw my profile under the heading, "The Ultimate Challenge". I cringed at the title. My responses to the questions were a verbatim account:

> That is a challenge, for me to walk is a mountain to climb. My right leg is slowly, slowly getting to operate. My left leg is not, but I am working on it. I can stand with some assistance for a couple of minutes. Then it gets exhausting. The physiotherapist is considering a brace or some sort of cast if I was able to use my left. I would need to have a raised heel on my right shoe. I am doing physiotherapy once a week, and part of that physiotherapy is to strengthen my legs.

I swallowed with a dry throat. I was surprised at the ease and honesty of my language.

> I've seen a side to people I wouldn't have otherwise seen if not for the accident … I want to progress, I want to get on with life. My Mum and Dad live ten minutes away and they help me out as much as I want them to. I don't want them to help me too much, I don't want to be treated like a child. Mum reminded me of my stubbornness to be left alone, "When you were young, you didn't want anyone to help you," she said.

I laughed. I imagined the tone my voice projected during the interview.

"I don't want anyone to feel sorry for me. I want to be treated like any other person in the Force, to be treated as an individual, not a person in a chair. And, unfortunately, it takes a person like me to tell them."

A leg calliper was made for my left leg. The device weighed about five kilograms and was made of metal and carbon fibre. I stared at it… "Please be gentle with me." A metal bracket held the left knee in place to aid my walk. The calliper was concealed beneath my jeans to attain a sense of dignity. To sit, I had to release the coupling so the knee could flex. With hand railings on either side at waist height, I stood up and moved my right leg, then the left, and right again. It had been about five years since I last stood upright, and now I was taking small steps, one foot after the other. Something that had come naturally to me before the accident was now a renewed wonder. A 20 mm raised heel was added to the underside of my right shoe to improve my walking gait. The calliper, though sturdy in support, felt robot-like with each stride.

"Keep going, Mike," said Gavin.

I moved my left leg again. "Fuuu…" I said with exasperation.

"Well done, keep going."

I walked around the house wearing the calliper with the aid of forearm crutches, fatiguing after ten minutes or thereabouts. I was still attached to my wheelchair. A part of me didn't want to depart from it. I considered it like my adult security blanket.

Though Mum and Dad knew of my right leg moving, I kept my training to stand and walk to myself. I wanted to surprise them with my progress.

"See this, Mum? Dad?" I demonstrated the use of my calliper in the kitchen.

Dad's eyes widened, watching on with espresso in hand.

"I can lock it." I stood up with the help of crutches. "And unlock it," I said, sitting down again.

"Tsk." Mum approached and kissed my cheek. She stood back to examine me, placing a hand over her mouth. "You look like born again… Michelangelo."

Her words rang true. Though I'd experienced the depths of despair, I did feel a renewal of my individuality. The light had cleared the way forward so much that I could see; to sing in the dark, to laugh at adversity, to live in hope. I extended my left leg and fixed the brace. "I'm going to the lounge room now." I smiled.

"Ok, Michal," Mum said, clasping her hands over her chest.

Dad's eyes followed my legs as I moved like a newborn giraffe.

"Be careful," Mum interjected.

I glanced at Dad. Tears pooled in his eyes.

The metal binding made a clinking sound with each stride. I could feel their thoughts trained on me: *How lucky are we to have Michael alive and walking?*

European Summer

I was entitled to long service leave in 1998. A European summer beckoned. I wanted to reclaim a sense of self by taking my leave in May, to live out the dream of long ago, before the fateful day of 16 April 1993. I likened the decision to being an escape, an adult version of my "time out" in the school chapel.

I looked forward to being a stranger: not a policeman, not a son, brother or mate. Simple anonymity. I'd be touring Europe alone, in my wheelchair and hire car.

The plane trip didn't start as I had hoped it would. Hours into the flight, somewhere over the Malacca straits, after helping myself to a variety of alcoholic drinks and enjoying *The Big Lebowski* I noticed my bladder filling up. *Oh shit… not now.* I looked down at the empty urine bag. A shot of adrenaline coursed through me. A blocked catheter was confirmed. I notified the stewards of the situation. If the catheter changeover was unsuccessful, the pilot was prepared to take an emergency detour and fly to Kuala Lumpur. A broadcast over the PA by the captain notified the passengers of my situation. I thought of the zany scenes from *Flying High* for amusement and to distract myself from the embarrassment.

"Did I pack an extra catheter in my backpack?" I quietly asked myself. I found one buried between the folds of the backpack. I had failed to pack a sterile water bottle but luckily found a syringe in my bag to deflate the catheter balloon. Beads of sweat ran down the middle of my chest. I asked the flight attendants to bring me boiled water in a cup. I sat still with my trousers down on the toilet seat as turbulence threatened to dislodge the sterile cup of hot water. I withdrew the 10 millilitres from the balloon that kept my catheter in place. My hands started shaking as I pulled gently to release the catheter. It failed to budge. I took a deep breath. Then, with effort, I tugged at the catheter. It dislodged from its fixture and slid out with urine flowing from it. *Thank you, God.* My trousers were soiled before I inserted the sterile catheter, passing through the layers of skin, muscle and bladder wall. I directed the flow of urine into the toilet. The sterile water hadn't cooled before I drew 10 mL of the boiled water into a syringe and injected it into the line inflating the balloon to hold the catheter in place. I felt the burning sensation against my bladder wall.

There was a knock on the door. "Are you ok, Michael?" the flight steward asked.

"Ah, yeah. I just need to change my trousers."

I changed into my clean pants and watched the remainder of *The Big Labowski* in the comfort of my seat.

I navigated around Ireland and the United Kingdom. I crossed the channel and drove around Europe. I toured thousands of kilometres, stopping at places of interest; me and my trusty wheelchair.

In a Donegal inn, behind closed doors, I had the privilege to remain as an honoured guest with the housekeeper and solo guitarist, listening to Irish ballads sung with gusto. Soho

London was my place to hang out. Plenty of bookstores at hand. My love for the laissez-faire lifestyle of Paris was sparked by the booksellers – or *bouquinistes* as they are locally known – along the Seine, with their postcards of chic Brigitte Bardot in 60s attire, and erotic literature on show. The pairs of storks nesting on white church towers along the Algarve coast of Portugal, and Seville's summer nightlife – a rustic bar with the sound of flamenco guitars – are memories that will remain. The orange-red buildings of the eternal city set ablaze by the afternoon sun were a sight to marvel at. I was transfixed by the ageless beauty of the masonry. The umbrella trees complemented the city's architecture. I fell in love with Rome. I was mesmerised by the stretch of glaciers in the Swiss Alps in the middle of summer as I drove higher and higher. The green hillsides and mountain range reminded me of *The Sound of Music*, the memory of sitting with Mum and Dad in the loungeroom, watching Julie Andrews singing *"The Hills Are Alive"*, made me smile.

For the record, Napoli is a city close to my heart. But one night I found myself in an area no tourist should accidentally venture into. I had been warned about the seedy side of Naples, but I was lost and needed to find my bearings. I parked my car in a rundown part of the city, with dilapidated buildings – and their occupants – eyeing me with suspicion. I wound down the window to aerate the car when I heard a man's voice call out, "Don Michele." I looked around to see where it came from. My immediate thought was the mafia. Then two young men appeared, one tallish man bearing a scar on his cheek, the other a short, stocky guy with rolled-up sleeves and clenched fists. They approached my driver's side door. No smiles, just straight-faced.

"Buon giorno," I said in my mother's dialect.

A nod of the head was the reply from Shorty. The one with the scar held out his hand and indicated with his fingers that they wanted cash. It was protection money or space for hire, I figured.

I nodded my head, "Ok." I opened the door, took out the wheelchair frame, connected the wheels to the frame's axle, placed the cushion on the seat and levered the brakes.

I looked up at them and smiled. I saw their expressions of surprise. Both stood back, made the sign of the cross and walked away. The encounter didn't scare me, though I found it slightly amusing afterward. I believed that no harm would come to me due to my disability, all the while I was prepared to hand over the cash they demanded of me. I had a feeling they'd have empathy for the *"povero Cristiano* (poor Christian soul)," as Mum would say of the less fortunate.

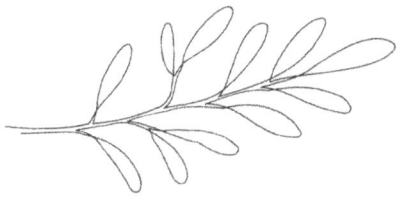

Purple Flesh

The urinary tract infections persisted after I got back home from my trip. It was August and I was sitting at my work desk typing a report when nerve pain in my testes started. *He has a sick sense of humour, the one with the pitchfork.* It developed into shooting pain from the legs to the soles of my feet. I started to sweat and developed nausea, accompanied by a sense of bladder fullness. The solution was to change the indwelling catheter urgently. I searched my backpack for a fresh catheter encased in a plastic sleeve, and the surgical kit to replace it with. *Oh fuck.* I'd forgotten to pack a replacement catheter. Beads of sweat ran down my back and chest. I wheeled toward the exit door. The steel handle, which stretched to the floor, caught my wheel as I attempted to leave the office. I went back and forth with my wheelchair, trying to free myself. "Fuuuck," I muttered under my breath.

Maureen popped up from behind the partition like a meerkat. "You right, Michael?" she asked, taking off her reading glasses.

"I don't know yet, Maurs." I managed to free myself. "I'll let you know later." I made my way to the nearest toilet, squeezed past the cubicle frame and pulled down my tracksuit pants to expose the stoma. The site was red and swollen to the point of bursting. I lifted the cuff of my trousers and saw the leg bag holding 10 millilitres of rusty urine. I tugged the catheter near the base, twisting it sideways and clockwise to break up crystals formed at the neck of the bladder. "Horse shit, cranberry juice prevents infections," I muttered. I narrowed my vision on the clear plastic tube. "C'mon… piss will ya." I watched the few drops of urine running down the tube. "You're an idiot, Michael."

I wheeled back to the office, my face feeling the heat of anxiety, and my eyes watering from the discomfort. I looked up at Maureen. "Looks like I need to go home Maurs," I said, wheeling past.

I knocked on Rod's door.

"Come in," Rod said.

I pushed my wheelchair with effort into Rod's office and doubled over.

"Mr Tarulli, what can I do for you?"

I let out a deep breath, "Boss, I don't have a spare catheter." I pointed to the stoma site. "This one's blocked and I don't have a spare."

He frowned. "Ok," he said, clenching his hands on the desk. "Do you need to go to the hospital?"

"Nah." My hands trembled on the wheelchair. "But I need to go home and change the catheter."

He stood up from his chair. "I'll organise police transport to take you home straight away."

A police car pulled up, parked on the curb in front of me. The driver stepped out – it was Sergeant Donnelly. My memory of him merged with the feeling of unease. I worked with

Donnelly during my time at City Patrol on the van. He was a tall, heavy-set man who stooped as he walked. He had blank, steely eyes that intimidated me. He bragged about the good old days, wielding the baton on the backs of crooks and placing Yellow Pages on the chests of criminals during interrogations. Donnelly looked at me without a word, just silence. His eyes softened on this occasion, or maybe he was getting older and tired.

Andy had accompanied me to the car. "You right Mick?" he said, helping me to the front passenger seat.

I dismantled the wheelchair by the curb. "I'm right, Andy."

"Ah, ya poor bugger," he said, shaking his head.

I closed the door and leant back with my eyes shut.

"Bass Street, Box Hill?" Donnelly said abruptly.

"Yep."

Donnelly stepped on the accelerator but stayed within the speed limit. The seatbelt around my waist was pressing against my bladder. I remained quiet. The build-up of fluid caused me to lean forward. Donnelly looked over at me. I sensed his helplessness.

"You've been working at the Youth Unit for long?"

I turned to him, "A few years."

He rubbed his neck. "What have they got you doin' there?"

I pressed my hand against my forehead, and then down the side of my face. "Reports and policy strategy."

"Interesting," he said with his bottom lip protruding. His eyes locked ahead in a hypnotic-like state. "And who's the officer in charge?"

"Rod… Norman." I grabbed the Jesus bar above my head. "Shit," I said sharply. I turned to my right again, Sergeant

Donnelly appeared unsettled, wiping his brow with a handkerchief.

"Does this happen to you a lot?"

I squeezed out a word, "Sometimes." I pushed my hands against the glove box compartment, my facial muscles contracting. "Fuck!" I blurted, more out of frustration with his badgering than from the pain.

"Unit 508, what's your ETA?" the D24 announcer said over the radio.

Donnelly turned to me. "How long you reckon from here?"

"About fifteen."

"VKC, this is 508, we're about fifteen minutes away."

I wanted to smash the car window with my fist. I clicked on the electronic gadget to force the window down. Sweat ran down the side of my temples, and my body odour overpowered the air rushing through the window.

We reached our destination. Donnelly got out of the car and handed me the wheelchair parts with haste. My hands shook as I pressed the wheels into the axle and unfolded the seat. I pivoted onto the wheelchair and rolled over bumps with the bladder feeling every inch of pain. I unlocked the front door and sped through to the bathroom. I deflated the balloon and pulled on the catheter. It wouldn't budge. "Oh, for fuck sake!" I yanked hard. The bloodied urine squirted out like a Cupid fountain pissing. I inserted a fresh catheter into the stoma and emptied the reservoir into the toilet.

"You okay?" Donnelly yelled out from the front door.

"I'm right." I looked at the used catheter and noticed at the tip a torn piece of purple flesh. I wasn't perturbed by this, more relieved. I figured it would heal over like a skin cut. It wasn't uncommon for a piece of inner skin to tear off when I performed a catheter changeover.

I wheeled out to the front door to meet Donnelly. He wiped his brow with a handkerchief. "You right now?"

I nodded my head. "Yeah." I scratched my brow. "You wanna drink?"

"Nah, I've gotta get back to the depot."

I was relieved to hear those words. Donnelly placed his hands in his trouser pockets, searching for his car keys. "Okay… I'll go then… take care."

I held onto the door, watching him walk away. He turned around and waved. I waved back.

I telephoned Rod, "Hi Boss."

"Is that the man of notoriously vicious and intemperate disposition?"

"Don't you forget it."

He laughed.

"I'm okay now, I did what I had to do."

"Good to hear. No need to come in tomorrow, if you're not up to it. Just behave yourself," he said with a chuckle.

Tomorrow's Fish and Chip Paper

A few weeks later, I received a telephone call at work from my solicitor, Mark McIntyre. He had represented me in my claim for common-law damages against the police department in 1997. The compensation was awarded for "pain and suffering" and "loss of earnings." Involved with the union bodies, Mark McIntyre was highly respected in the legal fraternity.

After our initial greetings, Mark proceeded to discuss the political agenda.

"I need to tell you, Mike; the state government is moving to change workers' rights."

His voice sounded urgent. I looked around to see who was within earshot. He laid out the government's proposal to remove the right to claim common-law damages for injuries deemed to be less than 30 per cent impaired, a considerable limit given up to 70 per cent of injuries failed to meet this threshold.

"Don't you think it's unfair?" he asked.

"Yeah, that's wrong."

"Listen. Are you interested in fronting a media conference with John Brumby? He's the opposition leader of the Labor Party"

I knew who he was. I paused. "Umm…"

"You'd be a perfect example, working as a police officer and injured on duty."

"Can I give it some thought?"

"Absolutely, young man."

I felt excited at the prospect of fronting the media. And nervous at being asked to stick my neck out, fearing the call to support my fellow workers on the front line would backfire on me. I ignored the bad feeling about it. I didn't want to disappoint McIntyre by declining the invite. It didn't dawn on me until later that Mark had a lot at stake from a business perspective if the proposed changes went ahead. The foolhardy in me couldn't resist; I wanted to prove to myself, and the world, that I was up for the fight. To face the media was an opportunity to feel important, like I belonged to a cause. I stewed on it for a few hours then picked up the phone and called Mark. "Yep, I'll do it."

"Great," he said with an upbeat tone. "We'll have a car come and pick you up tomorrow at eight in the morning. Oh, do you have a suit?"

"Yes."

"You'll need to wear it for the press interview."

The next day a black Holden Caprice drove into my driveway. A chauffeur, with hat and gloves, welcomed me to the front passenger seat. I sensed the task ahead would prove far beyond my understanding.

At Parliament House, I entered a room with decorated cornices and low-hanging lights. There, standing in front of me, was Mark McIntyre, and a man with a face familiar from the nightly news.

"Pleased to meet you," he said, shaking my hand. "John Brumby."

"Hi. Michael Tarulli."

He took to his chair and sat next to me. "I heard about your remarkable story of survival. Mark told me all about you. You were injured on police duty?"

I felt my face flush. I hated retelling the story. "Yes, it was in response to a 'shots fired' call. The accident almost claimed my life, and I've worked hard to get to where I am now."

He nodded in sympathy. "I'm sure you have, and it's a credit to you for how far you've come. We're pleased to have you." He smiled like the politician he was. "Have you ever done a press interview before?" he asked, adjusting his necktie.

"No, I haven't."

"No need to be intimidated by 'em. You'll be fine."

A woman interrupted us, handing him a sheet of paper.

Brumby looked over each page while scratching his chin. He took in a deep breath and exhaled slowly, then turned to me. "Good luck, young fella."

We moved to a room where tall tripod lights and large cameras sat on each side of us. Journalists, with their pens and notes, were at the ready, sitting in the middle of the studio. The desk acted as a protective barrier between us and the waiting media. My hands began to shake as Brumby, sitting beside me, delivered his views opposing the government's policies. He spoke at length and with confidence. My body started to shake as sweat accumulated under my armpits. A young male reporter stared, his expression intensified as he spoke to me. I saw his mouth open and close in quick succession. I heard the sound of words coming from his mouth, but I failed to understand the question in its entirety.

"Sorry, can you repeat the question?"

"What are your opinions of the proposed changes? And how does that affect your position as a police officer?"

The gallery watched on, waiting for my reply.

"We're under-resourced, which is putting our police officers at risk. We need better equipment to meet the demands of modern policing. We are still using old and unreliable equipment." I hesitated. "There are these heavy utility belts we call 'bat belts', every tool of the trade hangs off you. The belt digs into your hips and rubs against the skin causing red marks to appear. Carrying that with you all day is torture."

The gallery looked amused.

"Have you anything to say to the premier about the proposed changes?"

The adrenaline coursed through my veins. "Yes." I raised my finger in the air, "I invite Premier Jeff Kennett to sit down with me to chat about what it's like to be in my shoes." I stared intently. "The injuries can also be hidden… has he thought about that?"

The gallery went quiet. The reporters scribbled madly on their notepads.

After the press conference, we retired to a nicely decorated back room where tea was being served.

Brumby turned to me. "You handled yourself better than me at my first interview." He set his teacup down. "I liked your invitation bit." He smirked while adjusting his tie.

I felt my face flush, worried whether I'd said the right words or not. I excused myself and moved my chariot to the adjoining courtyard. The grey skies above matched the drab concrete slabs beneath my wheelchair. I bent forward with elbows on my knees, breathing deeply through my nose, feeling the build-up of blood behind my eyeballs. I lit up a cigarette and watched from afar as the journalists loitered around the corridor. I kept my distance to find quiet thoughts. My hand started shaking. I placed my free hand under my leg to calm myself. Each puff drew a cough, the ciggie hadn't reached halfway before my lungs screamed out for me to stop. I loosened the tie around my neck and took out a handkerchief to clear the mucus from my mouth. I looked up to see if anyone noticed. *Get me out of here.*

The six o'clock night news featured our press conference. The first thing I noticed were the strands of hair sticking up from my head like a cockatoo. I failed to hear what I was saying. *Why didn't anyone tell me my hair was up like that?*

The next day when I arrived at work, the phone on my desk rang. "Young Tarulli, see me in my office." Rod Norman sounded different from his usual cheerful self.

I wheeled into the office.

"I'm here, the man of notorious disposition reporting."

"Close the door behind you," he said.

I did as commanded. Andy Walsh stood with his hands behind his back, leaning against the office wall.

"G'day, Andy," I said, sensing trouble.

"Mick," he said, chewing away on his gum. The mood in the room reminded me of visiting the principal's office at school.

"We've had a call from the Chief Commissioner." Rod darted a look at Andy. "He wanted to reprimand you for your performance last night." The temperature under my shirt increased a few degrees. "You had no authority to go public on internal matters," Rod said with a sharp tone.

"Sorry, Boss," I looked away, staring at the wooden desk, noticing a chip on the corner's edge.

"Not to worry," he said calmly. "Just don't do it again."

"I won't, Boss." I picked at the chip with my thumbnail.

"What's the saying?" Rod turned to Andy. "Today's news is tomorrow's fish and chip paper?"

"That's it," Andy said, nodding his head.

"Ok, you can go now," Rod said with a relaxed smile.

"Thanks, Boss." I turned my chair around and accidentally caught Andy's ankle with the footplate. "Shit, sorry Andy."

"You're right, mate." He opened the door and followed me out of the office.

I mulled over the rebuke at my work desk, questioning whether I'd been wronged for supporting my colleagues, or if I acted out of character to seek attention driven by harboured anger. I was a whirlpool of mixed thoughts and emotions. I called Chris Haggarty. "Mate, I've been in the shit over my comments on TV last night."

"Umm, yeah – probably wasn't the smartest thing to do."

I blushed. "I know that now."

"Has Rod got your back?"

"Yeah… he has."

"Well, you won't do that again, my friend."

"I know, but they still piss me off. I don't trust any of them. Fuck'n bullshit, mate."

"Michael, just let it go."

Senior Constable

It was September 1999 – not long after Labor's Steve Bracks dispatched Kennett's Liberals in the state election – when I received a phone call from Rod Norman.

"Young Tarulli, can you see me in my office?"

What have I done this time?

I entered Rod's office. "Here on your command."

"Superintendent Crowley wants to see you in his office at 1400 hours, today."

"Ok," I said with hesitation. "Any reason why?"

"You'll find out soon," he said with a smirk. "He wants to have a chat with you."

I had heard about Superintendent Crowley, he was feared for his uncompromising and ruthless nature. He once sacked a Sergeant on the spot purportedly for misconduct. The sacked Sergeant had worked in our unit.

I approached Mr Crowley's office at the specified time.

"Reporting to see Mr Crowley," I said to the secretary.

"Your name?"
"Michael Tarulli."
"Take a seat, I'll let him know."
I am sitting down.

She hung up the telephone. "You can go in now."

I knocked on the door before entering.

"Come in." His voice was deep and measured. I opened the door and wheeled through into his office. He studied my movement with a deadpan expression. I positioned my chair in front of his desk. He looked fit for a man in his sixties, hair neatly combed to the side. The silver pips on his shoulders made him all the more intimidating.

"How are you, young man?"

"Good, Sir."

He picked up a folder and opened to the first page, studied it, and then proceeded to the second and third. My throat felt dry; I swallowed to moisten it.

"How long have you been with the Youth Advisory Unit?" He said without making eye contact.

I raised my eyes to think. "I arrived in '95."

"You enjoying the work?"

"Yes, I am, Sir."

"I see you completed the Crime Analyst course."

"Yes, I did, Sir." The Primary Analysis Course ran for two months at the Detective Training School. It covered theoretical examination and practical aspects of criminal intelligence analysis.

He looked up at me. "Rod Norman speaks highly of you."

I dared not reply, concealing my smile.

He moved in closer with elbows on the desk, wrinkles showing at the corners of his eyes. "It's time, son, you got out of the shabby clothes and looked decent."

I glanced down at my tracksuit and nodded my head in agreement. "Yes, Sir."

He pulled out a drawer and retrieved a wristwatch. "And you might want to get a haircut," he said with a firm tone, fixing the watch to his wrist.

I pressed my thumbnail into my palm. "Yes, Sir."

He stood up, walked over to the coat stand and grabbed his jacket. I admired the view from his office window, overlooking Flinders Street.

Turning to me, he said with a blunt voice, "I want you to wear the police uniform from now on. Look smart. You'll be receiving the Chief Commissioner's ten-year service medal."

"Yes, Sir."

I had anticipated this day. The thought of relinquishing my bohemian clothes and donning the uniform unsettled me. I was giving up my individuality, resigning to rules and regulations. I swallowed again.

"That'll be all, young man," he said, smiling with his lips pressed.

"Thank you, Sir." I turned my wheelchair around and left his office.

I thought about our meeting long afterwards. I believed he had my best interest at heart, and in his eyes valued me as a member of the Police Force. He had the balls to call it as he saw it, and for that, he got my respect.

I sat in my chair in the changeroom, overwhelmed by an empty feeling, unconvinced that the person looking back in the mirror reflected the truth. *Here I go again.* I was wearing the police uniform for the first time since the accident. The two stripes on my sleeve marked my rank: Senior Constable. I had passed the Senior Constable's exam during my tenure at Heidelberg and been promoted when a position for a Senior Constable had been advertised within the unit. The absence of identity left me feeling vulnerable and naked. I once believed that wearing the uniform was an extension of masculinity, bravery and approval. The truth was that I was fragile, frightened, and human. I wanted to protect the boy inside from the chaos outside. I wanted to listen to the endless music that once ignited the boy's soul.

I rolled my wheelchair into the office with my fresh uniform on show.

Maureen stood up from her chair and removed her glasses. "Michael, you look so handsome," she said with a glint in her eye.

"Thanks, Maureen." I felt the heat rise in my cheeks. I wheeled to the shelter of my cubicle to resume my research on youth crime.

Mr White

It was a hot December day when Maureen stood up and called out my name.

"Yes, Maurs?"

She wore a look of concern. "There's a gentleman on the phone who wants to talk to you. Something about his son being in trouble."

"Ok, put him through to me, extension 312."

I listened to the man's grievances. I encouraged him to report the crime at his local police station as we were non-operational.

"Please, Sir, I want to talk to you. I need your help," he said.

I took pity on Mr White and invited him in to hear his story. He had received death threats from a drug dealer who showed up at his front door wielding a sawn-off shotgun, demanding his son's whereabouts. The son owed the dealer a large sum of money.

Mr White took off his glasses and rubbed his eyes. "Officer, I've been trying to get David off the drugs." He wept. "He's mixed up with these people, bad people. Please, help me, officer?"

I placed my pen down on the notepad. "Mr White, I'll see what I can do. In the meantime, I suggest you move out of the house and stay somewhere safe."

He sniffled. "We're staying with my parents."

"Good." I reached out. "Here's my card with my number. And a list of support services for your son."

I drew in a deep breath. "I just need to ask you for time to dig into this, ok?"

He raised his reddened eyes to me. "Thank you."

I researched the database for known criminals who had the habit of using firearms, shotguns to be precise, and were in the business of drug dealing. I centred my enquiries within the southeastern suburbs. I went to the Bureau of Criminal Records and scanned through the file of a suspect I had in mind. I reflected on Mr White's statement.

"Arcan or Arken!" He kept repeating. "He said to me, 'Tell him Arken came to visit.'"

I placed the profile on top of the desk. The portrait of a guy with beady eyes and a goatee stared back at me. "Arkan" was his alias.

I received Rod Norman's approval to look into this, provided I conveyed what information I collated to the local C.I. (Criminal Investigation) branch. I invited Mr White to return to the office and view several profile photos of known criminals. I concealed each suspect's identity.

Mr White looked over each photo, page by page, scanning them with care.

"There," he said, pointing to the photo of Arkan. "That's him, I'm certain of it. I'll never forget those eyes."

I secured the intelligence report, marking it urgent, to the attention of Dandenong C.I. branch. I moved along the concourse between Building A and B, tapping the file back on my lap to prevent it from sliding off. I noticed a familiar face walking toward me as I picked up speed.

Graham Sinclair's eyes lit up, matching his elated smile. "Mr Tarully, looking mighty impressive in uniform."

I couldn't resist smiling. "Sir."

"It's Graham," he laughed. "Hey, how about we pay Mr Combie a visit?"

I froze, shocked at the thought of going to the Chief Commissioner's bunker.

"Come," he said with urgency, "Let's go see him."

My heartbeat quickened.

"He'd be happy to see you."

"Um… I've got to deliver an urgent report."

"It won't take long." He motioned with his head, "Follow me."

My mouth dried up and my throat tightened.

Graham pressed the button to the ninth floor as we entered the elevator. "Yes, Mr Combie will be pleased to see you."

The nerves got the better of me. I flicked the folder's edge with my thumb as Graham continued talking. *This is not happening.* Combie never came to visit me in the hospital, and I always wondered why. In a way, I was glad he didn't. I'd seen him on the news, the pressed lips, the creaseless face, the dreary monotone voice; he appeared cold and mannequin-like.

We exited the lift and passed by his secretary, who looked up from her desk.

"We're here to see Mr Combie," Graham said.

She watched me move along with curiosity, offering a faint smile.

Graham tapped on the Chief's door, "Mr Combie, we have company."

"Come in," the voice called from inside.

Graham opened the door and stepped aside, "Senior Constable Tarully is kind enough to pay us a visit," he said extending his arm out to me.

My heart punched against my ribcage as I entered the room. Mr Combie peered over his glasses, examining my every move. I inched closer to him. "Good afternoon, Sir," I said with a nod of the head.

He took off his spectacles, and, if I guessed right, he looked shocked. "Good afternoon," he said replying with a slight nod.

The room looked noticeably sanitised: rows of books placed in neat order, the carpet looked new, and the large wooden desk polished to a mirror finish.

"How good does he look in uniform, Mr Combie?"

The Chief glanced over my attire with steady eyes. "Indeed, a smart look, Mr Sinclair."

I clasped my hands in my lap, pressing and scratching the thumbnail into the opposite palm.

Mr Combie placed his pen aside and lay back in his chair. "How are you finding work at the Youth Advisory Unit?"

I took a deep breath before speaking. "It's been busy, Sir." I tried to imagine myself as Vito Corleone, appearing calm and in control; beneath the surface, I was shitting myself. "I'm managing just fine."

"Mr Norman is your supervisor, yes?" he said, swinging his reading glasses by one arm.

"Yes, Sir. He's been a stalwart of the unit."

"He's a good man, Rod Norman."

"He is." The seconds of silence became unbearable.

"How's your health?"

"I'm good, Sir. Some days are better than others."

"Good," he said nodding his head. "Very good."

There was a staring stand-off that went longer than I liked. And right then and there the thought came to me, which I suspected he read: *Why didn't you visit me in the hospital?*

"Ok, we'll leave you to your work, Mr Combie," said Graham, grabbing the door handle for our exit.

The Chief nodded.

"Sir," I said, with a steely smile, turning my wheelchair to exit.

It was the medal presentation day. I waited in trepidation for my name to be called out, removing lint from my trousers, and clearing the scuff marks off my shoes. The day before I had scrambled a tin of old shoe polish from the garage, cleaning the sad-looking leather shoes for hours. It brought back memories of the days at the Academy, although in those days I cleaned them to a mirror finish.

"Senior Constable Michael Tarulli," the speaker on the microphone called out, "for Diligent and Ethical Services."

They pronounced my name right. My nerves intensified with the congregation applauding as I made my way toward the front of the room. Assistant Commissioner Sinclair stood in full regalia with a medal in hand. *I'm getting there,* I thought, working over my wheelchair with my arms.

"Nothing gives me greater pleasure than rewarding you with this medal," Graham said, shaking my hand. "Congratulations, young man."

I felt like a child again, embarrassed and full of pride. It was the same feeling as when I shook Taka's hand after winning the nationals. "Thank you, Sir," I said, with a salute. And nothing gave me greater pleasure than receiving my award from the officer and gentleman who stood before me.

Call Me Tomorrow

Jase called out from over the fence, "Hey, Mike, want to come out to the Palmy tonight?" I rolled out to meet him. His head was visible above the fence line. "Taz and Deano are going," he said, tying his hair in a ponytail.

"Yeah, why not?"

We arrived at the Palmerston Hotel in Hawthorn. I sat on the barstool with Jase next to me. I picked up my glass of scotch, swirling the ice cubes around. "Remember that girl, Bridget, your model friend?"

Jase laughed. "Yeah, what about her?"

"Do you ever hear from her?"

"No, but you want to, don't ya?"

I laughed out loud. "Nah."

"Liar."

The night was long; the music became louder with increasing numbers of patrons at the bar and on the dance floor. I toyed with a beer coaster and looked up to see a familiar face on the other side of the bar. I felt like a fuse had been lit inside me. I began to heat up and the hairs on my arms prickled. Moyle had added a few extra kilos and lost his handsome appearance. He caught my eye.

"You fuck'n asshole," I said under my breath. I picked up my glass and swallowed the drink, slamming the empty tumbler down. "You fuck'n cunt."

Jase interjected. "Take it easy Mike, what's ya problem?"

My heart began beating faster, loud enough for my ears to notice. I leaned back on the stool and folded my arms, maintaining a dark stare. Moyle picked up his glass of beer and turned away.

"What's ya story?" Jase said.

"See that guy?" I said, pointing to Moyle. "He's the guy who drove the car."

"The guy in the brown jacket?"

"Yep." I slid off the barstool and onto my wheelchair. "I'm off to the toilet."

I rammed the door wide open with such force the young guy behind it stepped back in alarm. I bypassed him and entered the first cubicle, squeezing past the door frame. The dampness of piss on my hands didn't bother me, nor did the spray of shit in the porcelain bowl. I placed my left foot on the seat and released the valve to set free the urine.

I had learned that Moyle had acquired a licence to drive high-performance vehicles with the Traffic Operations Group. He had also escaped the clutches of the courts – the Department of Public Prosecutions dropped the serious traffic offences laid against him by the Accident Investigation Squad. "Not in the public's interest" were the words of the public prosecutor. The knife dug ever deeper.

The ruling reinforced my feelings of insignificance and justice denied. So many unanswered questions. Rumours like wounds that never healed, festering the layers of open skin.

"Fuck!" I yelled, punching the wall, twice, three times. Cracks appeared around the edges of the fist imprint. Urine spilt over my jeans, shoes and socks. "FUCK!" I pulled the end of the toilet paper with force and tore sheets to wipe down my shoes and trousers. I sat still as the emotions flowed from anxiety to anger, and back to anxiety. I wanted to face Moyle, yet fear got the better of me. I wheeled over to the mirror and looked into my eyes; the darkness hid within, born from years of learned discrimination and soul searching, the recurring pain of a damaged man. I saw the rim of a rifle's eye, zoning in on me.

I pushed my wheelchair through the forest of bodies on my return to the bar, my chest, shoulders and arms pumping with adrenaline. I parked the chair with the brakes on and rose up on my right leg, and then hoisted my weight onto the stool in one motion.

"Scotch, straight up," I called out to the barman.

"That guy came over," Jase said nervously. "He asked after ya."

I turned to Jase. "And?"

He held an anxious smile. "He wants to talk to you."

My heart thumped ever stronger against my ribs like beating drums increasing in volume. I tasted blood. "Yeah, well he can come up to me." I stared straight ahead, still as a statue. In the corner of my left eye, a figure appeared.

"Hey."

I turned to see Moyle standing there.

I was calm, like a bomb. "What do you want?"

"I wanna talk."

I held a cigarette between my thumb and forefinger, scowling with venom.

He continued, "I wanna talk about… what happened…"

The music from the speakers hit a pitch; I didn't catch his last words.

I turned to him. "Yeah? Well, I don't wanna talk right now. Best we talk when I'm sober." I reached over the bar and grabbed a pen and napkin. "This is my number," I slid the napkin in front of him. "Call me tomorrow."

He picked it up and left without a word.

I commenced shivering as I sucked on my cigarette.

"You okay?" Jase said.

I blew out a steady stream of smoke and shrugged my shoulders.

Jase continued to speak. I failed to take in his words. I was stuck in a vault, unable to free myself from where I sat. The hours went by and still I sat rooted, feeling numb.

"Mike, you right?" Jase said. "Let's go, yeah?"

"Nah, I'm stayin'."

Jase grabbed my wheelchair, waiting for me to take my seat. "C'mon man, let's go."

I looked at him. "No, I'm stayin'."

I continued drinking until the call for the last drinks. I ventured out into the morning light; the sun was doing its best to break through the clouds. The wheelchair felt like a truck. I laboured to push forward with my shoulders and hands. The city came alive with businessmen walking with cups of coffee in hand and tradespeople driving with elbows resting on the driver's open window frame. People watched me, studied me, peeled layers off me. *What the fuck are you looking at?*

"Why," I asked myself. "Why is this all happening to me?" The emotions continued to swirl, trembling to my very core. I looked up to the heavens. "Why me?" The wall finally breached. I slumped against the brick wall of a rundown motor repair shop, holding tight to the wheelchair to steady myself. Endless tears streamed down my cheeks. My insides felt like they shrank in on themselves. I sobbed like a child. A couple walked toward me, they looked to be in their sixties.

"Are you ok?" The woman said, holding a hand to her chest.

I looked up with watery eyes, seeking a human softness to connect with. "I had a car accident." I caught my breath to spill my confession. "I can't cope with this anymore."

She placed a hand on my shoulder. "Oh, love, we lost our daughter in a car accident."

I looked up at her. "I'm so sorry for your loss."

"Would you like us to help you?"

I shook my head, "No, thank you."

The husband and wife turned to each other. She bent down and met me at eye level, "Look after yourself, won't you?"

I wiped the tears from my eyes. "I will," I said, lifting my cheek muscles to smile. The pair walked on, glancing back now and then before disappearing around the corner.

I sat still. The soft smell of spring brought back childhood memories of cherry blossoms and bursting acacias. A wattlebird clucked nearby; sparrows, in their numbers, landed at my feet, pitching their high notes as they skipped along the ground. Sunlight breached the clouds in all its glory. I closed my eyes, the deep breathing echoed in the heart's chamber. A golden carefree moment I wanted to last forever. The precious hold slipped as the silence was broken by barking dogs. The edges darkened and the clouds gathered. I succumbed to the throws of dark cruelty.

I wheeled to the curb, hailing a taxi to take me to Dr Michael Maloney's office. I arrived at the clinic with sapped energy levels.

"Can I help you?" The young receptionist asked softly.
"I like to see… Dr Maloney… please?"
"You have an appointment?"
"No." A second wave overcame me. I wept, resting my head on my arm from sheer exhaustion.
She offered me a cup of water. "I'll let Dr Maloney know you're here."
I raised my eyes to meet hers. "Thank you."

Michael admitted me to the rehabilitation centre for overnight observation. After my discharge, I waited for that phone call from Moyle. Days passed and I knew the call would never come. I felt relieved.

No Better Than the Greyhounds

Chris and his wife, Alyson, relocated back to Melbourne about a month after my run-in with Moyle. I met up with Chris on a Saturday afternoon at the Mitcham Hotel, where punters gathered to bet on the races.

"I've got a hot tip for race four at Caulfield," Chris said getting up from our dining table, "Comin' over for a flutter?"

"I'll come with ya, but I won't bet."

He cleared his throat. "You wanna beer?"

I put my thumb up, "Yep."

I took up a position under the TV screens where races from Randwick, Morphettville and Caulfield were feeding live action.

"Go! Go! C'mon, girl! Go! Go!" a man kept yelling from behind as the horses galloped down the straight. His irate voice continued, "Don't get boxed in!"

I turned to see a rotund, red-faced man, with sticky saliva hanging off his lips.

"Yeah, baby!" he yelled as the horses crossed the finish line.

Chris arrived with two pots of beer, placing them in the centre of our table. I stared back at the sports screen and noticed the greyhound races on another monitor. *It's nighttime somewhere in the world.* I watched the lean sprinters chase a mechanical stuffed rabbit around a track. Round the circuit they went, bumping each other out of position.

"It's a dummy, my furry friends, don't fall for it."

"Michael, they're trained to chase the dummy rabbit," Chris said sarcastically, ripping open the packet of salt and vinegar crisps.

I turned to him. "I wish they were smart enough to know the difference."

"They're chasing an illusion." Chris chuckled, "We're no different, Michael."

I looked at him, seeking clarification of the remark. He ignored my eyes, too busy staring at the screen with his wager in hand.

"And they're off, for the Caulfield Guineas…" said the race-caller over the speakers.

I looked up at the screen and watched a jumble of racehorses galloping against the railing. I turned my attention back to the greyhounds. A shiver ran up my spine: I was no better than the greyhounds – but instead of a rabbit, I was chasing an illusion. And I was no better than the racehorses at the mercy of the rider's whip; forced to travel on a fool's path under the weight of command. *How long will it be before I give the job away?* I reflected on the time I crossed paths with Kath Daly in the food hall. I remembered her words, "Michael, I would never have thought of you as a policeman, it's not you." I lay my hands on my head and let out a deep breath. *She was right. I've been living a lie. I've reached the bottom line. It's time to pry off the shackles and set off on another path.*

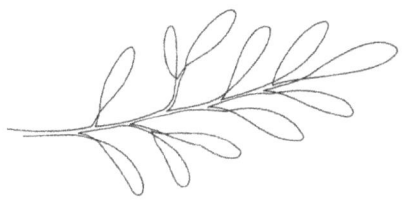

Man of Notorious Disposition

After consulting with Michael Maloney, it was an easy decision to make. I knew deep down it was the right way to go. I wanted to start anew. I wanted to be free. I wanted to be a stranger to the police department and those connected to it. I expressed my desire to Rod Norman to have a small gathering for my farewell party. And so, on the day of my final goodbye, I would start my life as a stranger to the police.

I squirmed in the wheelchair, trying to find an inch of comfort. The pain hammered at my sitting bones while I remained still. I twisted the paper napkin around my index finger until the tip became numb. I turned and smiled at my colleagues, watching their lips move in conversation – meaningless words. I wheeled to the corner of the room.

Andy followed and stood beside me, placing his bear-like hand on my shoulder. "You okay, champ?"

I looked up at him. "Yeah, all good, mate."

"You've done a great job, Mick, we'll miss ya heaps."

"Thanks, mate," I said sheepishly.

I felt like I hadn't achieved much at all; filing papers and typing reports wasn't worth the accolade.

Rod Norman stood at the front of the room. "Can I please have your attention?" he bellowed to the crowd. "Can I ask Michael Tarulli to come up to the front?"

I pushed my wheelchair forward to the front stage, hands pressing hard on the wheels.

He glanced down at me as I approached. "Young Tarulli."

I positioned my chair next to him and folded my arms with my head bowed.

"Man of notoriously vicious and intemperate disposition. You, ok?" he said as a joke.

A few of the audience chuckled.

I looked up with a forced smile, "Yep." My cheeks felt a rising heat.

"We're privileged to have seen the positive changes you've made at the Youth Advisory Unit. I've received testimonials from magistrates and youth workers praising your efforts over the years."

I willed myself to face the crowd to show appreciation.

"We know you've been through a lot, and it's a testament to your character the way you've carried yourself."

The gnawing pain from the base of my skull to the coccyx ate away.

"It was a privilege to have you working with us and please accept this token of our appreciation for your years of devoted service."

I smiled with awkwardness as the crowd applauded. I looked at the wooden plaque. The caption read, *To the man of notorious disposition, we say thank you, Victoria Police Youth Advisory Unit. 18 December 2000.*

"And here is another gift for ya, Mick," Andy said, presenting me with a coffee mug with the Victoria Police emblem on it.

The last thing I need, I thought as I inspected it. I smiled at him, and at Rod. "Thank you, guys." I turned to the crowd. "Well... I enjoyed my time working with you all... fond memories I'll keep forever... um," I placed the mug onto the plaque, "So yeah, thank you for the gifts and keep doing the good work."

The applause seemed to go on forever. I locked eyes with Maureen, she leaned her head to one side and smiled with tears in her eyes.

The crowd assembled around the table for cut sandwiches and alcoholic beverages.

Maureen stepped forward, squeezing past Rod and Andy. "Oh Michael, so sad to see you go. We'll have to catch up for coffee sometime."

"Yes Maureen, that'd be great."

The hum of voices in the room became too much. "Excuse me, all, I'm going to the toilet," I said, grabbing my lower back.

I headed straight to the handbasin. I cupped my hands under warm water, wishing for asylum on some rainbow island. I looked at myself in the mirror, ten-year-old Michael stared back at me. My lips trembled. The tears held off. I turned toward the cubicles, screwed up my nose and frowned. I pushed open the first door and faced a bowl of sprayed faeces. I entered the adjoining toilet to find urine and wet toilet paper on the floor. The last toilet was clean enough, except for the brown smudge at the base. I lifted my lower leg onto the plastic seat with both hands. The latex bag had taken on the shape of the

Hindenburg, its stretched Velcro straps had marked my skin. I opened the valve and watched the silty urine escape; like aged cheese, the smell caused my nose to scrunch.

An electric shock ran down my leg. "Jesus! Not again." I tried steadying to avoid a urine spill over my shoe. The pain continued in waves. I dug my fingernails into the skin to numb the pain. *He's at it again with the pitchfork.* I ripped off a sheet of toilet paper and wiped the spilt urine from the seat.

Rod and Andy watched me wheeling toward them.

"Here he comes, legend," Andy called out.

Rod looked at me with a frown, "You okay, young Tarulli?"

"Struggling a bit boss."

"Do you want us to take you home?" he said.

"Nah, I'm catchin' the train. Thanks anyway."

"You sure? We can organise one of the boys to drive ya home."

"Nah, I'm right." I looked at Rod. "Really, I'll be fine. I prefer the train ride anyway."

My hands pressed hard on the tyres up against the exit door, it proved rigid. I tried again, using my wheelchair like a battering ram.

"Here, mate," Andy said, pushing the door wide open. "There ya go."

"Bloody door doesn't like me," I said disguising my embarrassment.

"See you, Mick," Andy shouted as I moved my chair along the footpath.

I put my hand up, "See ya, mate."

"Hey, Mick?"

I turned my chair around to face him.

"Ya Mum and Dad would be proud of you."

"They are mate." I gave a thumbs-up.

"Hey, Mick!"

I turned around again.

Andy flexed his right bicep like Arnold Schwarzenegger. "Stay strong."

I laughed, replying with a double bicep flex. I turned around and wheeled along the city streets with renewed enthusiasm. The nerve pain gnawed away. My hands gripped the tyres, pushing and steering left to right and vice versa. The air swept over my face. Pedestrians became obstacles, and I brushed past them with my arms and shoulders. My calloused hands gathered every inch of road grease and food stains.

I approached the intersection of Russell Street and Flinders Lane. The red man flashed, telling me to stop. A wind gust carried the smell of putrid waste from industrial bins nearby, bringing back memories of my time at City Patrol. I was a fresh-faced twenty-two-year-old lad, who had just graduated from the Academy in 1989. I set out patrolling the city streets at night, in the hours when humanity revealed its vulnerability. The city was a harbour for lost souls with the continuous vibration of melancholy. "Shoebox man" lived under a row of sturdy cardboard boxes in Hardware Lane. His skin was so pale and dry, he looked like an embalmed corpse. When I passed, he'd look at me with distant eyes. We harboured a mutual tolerance for one another. He appeared unbothered by the smell of vegetable waste and rotten fish. What drove him to live in such a world?

Tommy was a delinquent teen who roamed the streets. *No fixed place of address*, I wrote in my notebook. He'd been recorded for burglary and theft. When I questioned him, at his hangout in Swanston Street, he'd point to the inverted pentagram on my police hat. "That's the mark of Satan," he said with a laugh, revealing missing front teeth. How did it come to pass for a father to kick his son out of home?

One night there was a pretty, red-haired girl lying unconscious on the cold pavement in Flinders Lane, exposed to the immorality of a dark city. I tried to rouse her from her sleep by shaking her. Her breathing was shallow, her pupils had the appearance of "drug eyes", she was alive. But not. I held her cold hand to feel a faint pulse. "Radio for an ambulance," I instructed Smitty, with haste. He, too, was a junior. I took off my police-issue jacket and placed it under her head. "Hang in there," I said, close to her ear. "The ambulance is on its way."

She didn't have identification on her, she was an unknown. The ambulance crew arrived. "Wake up for me," the ambulance officer pleaded with her, administering some liquid into her vein. Her eyes slowly came to life. "Can you tell me your name?" He continued, "Can you tell me where you live?" she mumbled, moving like a rag doll in the arms of his female companion. "Ok, let's lay you down in the back of the ambulance."

I wonder what became of her.

The day shift was different. I avoided eye contact with men in suits and those wearing hard hats. Their silent stares unnerved me, so I scanned the bluestone pavement with its moonlike pockmarks instead.

"Look up, Tarully," said the Sergeant. I much preferred the night shift.

I rested my attention on the present moment, taking in a deep breath as the red signal man stared at me. The pedestrians crowded around, making it an uncomfortable wait. I steadied the wheelchair before the red man turned to the green man. I'm free.

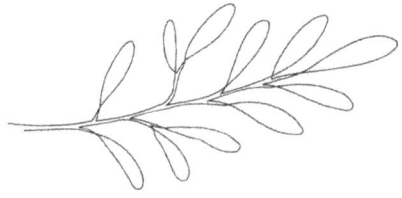

Love Letters and Poems

I sat in my parents' kitchen, the room where we spoke our truth. With my back against the wall, I released the fixed brace that kept my left leg straight to flex my knee. The velcro straps irritated the skin so much so that I removed the device from under my tracksuit pants and scratched away at it. I took pleasure in soaking up the smell of *sugo di pomodoro*. Mum sat opposite me, waiting for the sauce to reach its optimal temperature to complement the pasta. The view of the garden with its rows of tomato plants, laden with ripe fruit, served as a distraction to the unanswered questions.

"Michal, why you finish wid de police?" Mum asked, smiling half-heartedly. I turned to Dad who looked at me, he too appeared interested in my explanation.

"Mum, I couldn't sit for too long at work, there was too much pain in my lower back." I refrained from telling them that the complications of urinary infections and blocked catheters didn't help either. I couldn't admit the fact that I didn't enjoy police life. Instead of celebrating failure, I retreated into it.

"Okay, Michal." She drew a deep breath. "I just worry for you now."

Dad held onto a paper napkin, tongue rolling over his teeth to get rid of the gristle from the beef *braciole* (rolled beef slowly simmered in tomato sauce).

"I'll be okay, Mum, don't worry about me." I tapped my fingers on the laminated table. "Change is good... I'll do something else, like study, or work for myself." A long pause ensued. I lifted my head to catch her eye. "Mum, it's okay." I flexed my right bicep. "I'm strong, see?"

"Tsk, you make me laugh, Michelangelo."

Sunlight filtered through the neighbour's eucalyptus tree, catching Mum's face at an angle, light that I hoped would calm her. She got up from her chair, "You want cup of tea?"

"No thanks, Ma."

She walked toward the stove, checking the coffee pot as it started to steam at the spout. "Ah," she said, doubling back. "Before I forget, I want to show what I find when I clean de bedroom." Mum walked off, and I waited in anticipation.

"Michal, why don't you get a haircut?" Dad said, motioning with his fingers like they were scissors.

"Dad, please, give it a rest."

Mum came in carrying in her hands crumpled, folded old paper. "I move de bed and find dis paper, you know, under de wood. You put dere, Michal?"

I laughed; my stash of forgotten poems had resurfaced. "Yes, Mum, I put them under the bed legs." I unfolded each paper, coloured over time, and read the lines and stanzas of my thoughts and feelings; adolescent words of wisdom and advice for myself.

One was neatly folded over many layers. I knew what its contents would be. I scratched my head back and forth till the hair strands stood up. I'd written a love poem using a river as a metaphor. With the backdrop of mountains, I had drawn the river in pencil, meandering between them with the sunset in the background. The love poem was dedicated to Caroline. I would've been about eighteen or nineteen when I wrote it, lying on my bed. I felt the heat rise in me, the sensation borne out of anger for failing to win her heart. Understandably, I was gripped by fear of failure at the time. The coffee pot made its spluttering sound. Mum, standing at the stove, removed the pot from the burner with the aid of a tea towel and placed it on the table. I looked up to notice Dad staring at me. By the look in his eye, I could tell he wanted a running commentary about the paper's contents.

"Oh well," I said under my breath. "Nothing important, nothing new." Caroline was a distant memory. I folded the paper as small as possible and placed it in my pocket. My thoughts reverted to the love letters and poems I wrote to those I fell for; I counted and named them in my head. Most recipients replied with sentiments of "we can be friends".

I remembered a night, in my wheelchair, when after drinking copious amounts of alcohol at my Box Hill home, I gathered a different pile of papers – letters and poems of years gone by – from the drawer. I jammed them between my thighs and wheeled over the brick pavement of my backyard. I made a mound using twigs and dried leaves for the sacrificial burn. I levered my wheelchair brakes at the pile's edge and lit a matchstick, placing the burning head under the newspaper. The fire took hold and my hands trembled as I thought twice about my decision. Once the flames towered to a height, I just did it; I threw the letters and cards into the fire. I watched them darken and turn in on themselves as the fire consumed years of devoted words and affections, erasing my foolish deeds and false hopes. I took a deep drag of the cigarette and blew a steady stream of smoke into the evening air, surrendering to the night sky with its multitude of stars.

I sat on my chair, deep in thought of failed relationships. The more I tried to push through the feeling of ineptness, the more I agonised. *Maybe I was an evil warlord in a previous life. This now is hell as punishment. Maybe I was deceiving myself: I pushed a few suitors away, finding excuses not to follow through to the end goal. Maybe I was afraid she'd eventually see the cracks and scars I hid so well… Maybe I dithered for too long before she decided on someone else. Or simply the tea leaves didn't read right for me?* I felt as if an immovable force nullified any chance for me to find happiness; I was undeserving of the gift.

Mum poured hot coffee into Dad's cup. Dad wiped his lips with the napkin, readying himself for the fresh brew. The smell reminded me of when I was very young, sitting at the kitchen table; Dad sipping his coffee while we watched Mum mix ingredients for cheesecake, or roll the pin to make fresh pasta sheets. The memory pulled me back into all that was good and safe in the house; my heart reclaimed the finite moment of familiarity.

Bladder Reconstruction

Since the accident, my bladder had been the size of a tennis ball, having lost functionality from nerve damage. The suprapubic catheter was the cause of constant infections, and its removal became a priority. I needed an augmented bladder to reduce infection and accommodate a higher volume. The procedure was not without risks – the growth of ulcers on the bladder lining and benign tumours were a possibility.

Dr Alan Crosthwaite, my urologist, reassured me that the odds of complications were slim to none. He drew an image of a re-engineered bladder on a piece of paper.

"Why shouldn't I keep what I have now?" I asked. "I can manage the infections, no problem."

"A permanent indwelling catheter would do more harm in the long term." His eyes took on a softer tone. "Let me put it this way… if you were my son, I would recommend the procedure."

Browsing the internet, I found a similar case in England. A patient who had suffered pelvic trauma from a motor vehicle accident, also tore his urethra and underwent the procedure.

And a similar procedure had been completed in the United States.

I made my decision. The countdown to surgery began, rapidly moving from months to weeks to days. The fear grew as I prepared for another round with Mike Tyson.

"You, ok?" asked Alan through his surgical mask.

"Yes," I said, nodding.

He placed his hand on my arm and smiled with reassuring eyes. "You'll be fine."

I woke up to the burning sensation of a hot kettle sitting on my abdomen. I rubbed my eyes and noticed my enlarged abdomen, bloodied, with a line of stitches from the diaphragm to the pubis. I feared to move in case the sutures tore apart. The nurse placed the regulator to the IV drip into my hand. "If you are in pain release this valve. It will increase the morphine."

The operation was a success. The appendix acted as a canal, conveying urine from the bladder to the stoma (the exit hole in my belly button). The canal contained a valve to ensure one-way flow. Twenty centimetres of my large intestine was surgically grafted to the bladder wall to accommodate extra fluid. The urology nurse, Simone, gave instructions on how to use the catheter. I smothered the plastic tube with lubricant gel to enable the catheter to enter the stoma with ease. I still had trouble inserting it.

"Keep the pressure firmly on the catheter," Simone said encouragingly.

I forced the catheter through the stoma, the sensation was like inserting a screwdriver into the abdomen.

Simone watched my technique. "Well done Michael."

I observed urine fill the measuring jug. *It looks like ginger beer.*

Simone placed an instrument against my abdomen to detect bladder volume. If the machine beeped twice, there was a residue of urine, if it didn't beep at all, it was clear. The machine beeped twice, with the red-light flashing.

"You haven't emptied your bladder," she said.

I reinserted the catheter until the bladder was drained.

As days progressed to weeks and months, the screwdriver pain decreased.

New Beginnings

One night in April 2001, I arrived home to find fire trucks with their red lights flashing in the dark, parked outside my house. Marcello and Mirella stood in the driveway with arms folded, staring at me through the windscreen with shocked expressions. Heat radiated out onto my skin's surface.

"Really, why am I not surprised!" I said to God. "What is it this time? What are you trying to tell me?" I parked the car as Marcello and Mirella approached. I wound down the window.

"Michael, you're here!" Mirella said, sobbing. "You're ok."

I didn't reply. I watched the white smoke billow from my open roof and into the night sky.

"Where were you, Michael? We tried calling you."

My Nokia mobile had died. The smell of damp smoke filled the air. The "burring" sound of the fire truck filled my ears. It was pumping water to the attached hoses, dousing the lounge room of what was once my home. I got onto my wheelchair and sat on the edge of the nature strip, watching on as firefighters with flashlights went about their business.

I couldn't look Marcello or Mirella in the eye. "Where are Mum and Dad?" I asked.

"They're at home," Marcello replied.

I anticipated Mum and Dad's pain. They must've been wondering what curses had befallen me to deserve this. Chris and Alyson arrived, parking their car on the opposite side of the road. The forlorn looks on their faces turned to resolution once I'd spoken to them.

"How are ya mate?" Chris asked.

I threw my hands in the air.

Alyson placed her hand on my back and gently massaged it in a circular motion.

I sighed. "What the hell did I do to deserve this?"

A gentleman in a suit, holding a clipboard walked up to me. "Are you the owner of the property?"

"Yes."

"My name is Detective Barry from Box Hill C.I. Is your name Michael?"

"Yes… Michael Tarulli."

"Where have you been tonight, Michael?"

"Visiting a friend in Doncaster."

"What time did you leave your house?"

"Oh, around 4:30 pm."

"Did you go straight from your place to Doncaster?"

"Yes."

"And how long did you stay with your friend?"

"All night, until now."

He scribbled on his notepad.

"Who is your friend, and where does he or she live?"

"Sue lives at 9 Wunderee Avenue, Doncaster."

"Is this your car?" He pointed to my Falcon.

"Yes."

"Can you pop up your boot for me?"

Ok, I know where this is going. "Yeah, no worries."

He inspected the entire cabin, including the glove box and seats. A flame of anger flickered through my mind.

"Can I go and have a closer look?" I said to the detective. "I want to see my house."

He hesitated. "Yeah, sure. Follow me."

"You want us to come with you Michael?" Chris called out.

"No, I'm right."

I followed the detective along the stony path to the front door, guided by his flashlight.

"Watch your step."

I'm in a wheelchair.

The fire hoses strewn on the ground prevented my advancement to the front door. I caught a glimpse of the gutted lounge room, where I made out the bronze statue of Buddha sitting on the floor, untroubled and at peace. The wooden coffee table I had made was charred, barely recognisable. Firefighters scurried about, desecrating what was once my home with their boots and axes.

"Ok. I've had enough." I turned my wheelchair and headed out onto the street. I felt numb like I didn't know myself.

My neighbour, Dave, called out, "Mike!" His top half leaned over the fence. A man in his sixties, Dave had become my new next-door neighbour about a year prior, when Jase and company moved out.

I looked at him, embarrassed.

"Mike, thank Christ you're safe. I didn't know if you were at home. I called out to ya."

"Yeah." I hesitated. "I'm alright."

"I tried to hose down the flames mate," he said with laboured breath.

I shrugged my shoulders, not knowing what more I could say, and made my way back to where my siblings waited on the footpath.

Mirella's voice trembled. "Michael, stay overnight at my place. Or do you want to go to Marcello's?"

I shook my head.

"Do you want to go to Mum and Dad's place for the night?"

I looked up. "No, not Mum and Dad's." The thought of them suffering were like bullets to the torso.

"I'll stay with Chris and Alyson." I turned to them. "Is that alright?"

"Yes," Alyson replied, placing her hand over my shoulder.

I looked over at Mirella. "Please tell Mum and Dad I'm ok. I don't want them to worry."

I sat in the back seat of Chris's car. It was a quiet drive to their home in Kew. Alyson turned on the FM radio. The music spilt into the silence. Then "Burning Down the House" by Talking Heads came on. Chris and Alyson glanced at each other.

"How appropriate," I said with a chuckle.

Alyson changed the dial to another station.

I insisted on sleeping on the couch. All night I stared into the black space of the lounge room, hearing a creak now and then from the prevailing wind. The smell of wet smoke from my clothes kept me company.

It was morning.

"Do you want some tea, Michael?"

I sat up on the couch and ruffled my hair. "No, thanks, Alyson."

A knock sounded on the front door. Alyson walked from the kitchen to answer it. Morning light filled up the corridor.

"Hi, we're from Kew Police Station. We have orders to check on Michael Tarulli," a male voice said.

"Yes, come in."

I rubbed my eyes to make them lively. Two young male officers walked into the lounge room. We greeted each other. They asked how I was feeling and whether I needed anything. Alyson stood nearby, observing with caution.

"You have a child I see?" said one of the boys to Alyson, referring to a teddy bear dressed in a firefighter's costume. The soft toy sat at the foot of the TV.

"No, that's my husband's teddy." Chris was a volunteer firefighter.

The two officers looked at each other. I glanced over at Alyson. She looked at me with amusement.

"Um," one of the officers fidgeted with his hat. "We have instructions to take you to your house. The detectives want to question you further."

"Yeah, no worries." I slid onto my wheelchair. "Let's go."

We arrived to waiting media and police cars. I was assembling my wheelchair from the passenger's seat when a reporter with a microphone approached. "Michael, what do you have to say about the house fire?"

I didn't look at him, refusing to answer. Dressed in a white shirt and tie, Andy was suddenly standing between the reporter and me. The big fella had appeared like a breaching whale. "Ok, stand back. He's not talking to anyone."

I looked up and made eye contact with Andy.

"You right, Mick?"

"Yeah."

"Follow me, mate." He turned around and glared at the reporters whilst chewing gum. I was introduced to another detective.

"Detective Davies from Box Hill C.I."

My chair rolled forward before I could steady myself and shake his hand. "G'day."

"Do you prefer Michael or Mick?"

"Oh... don't care really."

"I need to ask some questions about the house fire last night."

"Yeah, no worries."

"You mind following me to the back of your house?"

I nodded my head in agreement. I looked at the charred skeleton of my home. The black wooden frames held their form. The front lounge was exposed to the sunlight for all to see. I pushed the chair up the ramp to the back patio and looked inside the kitchen. The whole interior was blackened, and the smell of wood death filled my nostrils. *This was once my home.*

"Michael."

I turned to the detective.

"Was the back door locked?"

"Yes, it's always locked before I go out. I always check it."

"You can see that it isn't," he said, demonstrating the sliding action of the door frame.

I looked at him casually, hiding my discontent. "It was locked."

I noticed broken glass on the ground, near the ferns. I looked up and saw louvres missing. "See that?" I pointed to the small window to the bathroom. "They removed the louvres from the bathroom window."

He walked over to take a closer inspection. "Do you know anything about that?"

I felt the anger rise – like a cat, my back was arched and I was ready to strike. "Well, it looks like the point of entry to me. Whoever it was obviously removed them to get in," I said, making it clear I was stating the obvious.

"It's quite high off the ground for a person to do so on his own." He turned to me. "Could you have arranged for people to break into your house while you were out?"

I didn't know whether he was joking. But the way he stared at me suggested he was not. I leaned forward and caught his eye. "No," I said emphatically. I understood the process of elimination, treating everyone as a suspect, and the questioning process. Detective Davies continued scribbling, detached from all emotion. I was just another number to him.

He stopped writing. "We think the fire started in the study, under your desk." He looked at me for a reaction. I didn't know what to say. I stared at the garden, the ferns, the palms, the bird of paradise. They all looked sad. The burnt odour consumed the floral scent.

It made sense to me. Whoever burgled my place and torched it did so out of spite. On the desk rested my retirement plaque. Piles of printing paper were placed beneath the desk. An accelerant was used to ignite the pile. The plaque was salvageable. Photos, books, clothes, and poems were all lost. To this day, I believe the burglars were from a residence a few houses down the street. Two guys in their twenties lived there and kept to themselves. One walked around with a hoodie, and his mate wore a baseball cap. We didn't interact, except for the odd hello or nod of the head in passing. I'd notice suspicious cars stopping out the front of their place after dark. A person would get out of the car and walk up to the side gate, return to the car minutes later and drive off. I suspected drug dealers. And I told this to Davies.

I was asked to attend the office of the insurance company. There to greet me in her private office was a former police officer, Sally Carney, who I'd worked with in my days at Caulfield Police. She was investigating my policy claim for compensation. I sat facing her across her desk; there was no warm welcome or talk of our policing days. Sally clenched her hands on the desk, and with a straight face she commenced. "Michael, we think you were responsible for the house fire. What do you have to say about that?"

"No. That's not true."

"The investigating officer with Victoria Police seems to think you are. What do you say about that?"

"No. That's not true."

"It's been known in the past that police officers have done this sort of thing. Set their house on fire to claim insurance money. What do you have to say about that?"

I clasped my hands and looked her dead in the eye. "Sally? You knew me well in my days at Caulfield. Do you think I would be capable of such a thing?"

She failed to meet my eyes from then on.

The investigation concluded. I was cleared of insurance fraud. I followed up with Detective Davies for any leads on the investigation, but weeks and months after nothing came to light. I spent my days in a rental flat in Mt Waverley, and later at Mum and Dad's house until my new place was built.

Every Saturday afternoon Andy and I would meet at our favourite café on Brunswick Street, Fitzroy. Here we discussed politics of the day and revised our failed relationships. It wasn't long after the house fire when I first met Russell "Rusty" Smith – a proud Pitjantjatjara man from Port Augusta, and a renowned musician. He and Andy had established a friendship through their work with disadvantaged young people.

Andy noticed Rusty walking along the footpath. "Russell," Andy called out with outstretched arms. "What brings ya down here?"

The stranger turned to meet him, flashing a magnetic smile "I followed your tracks, brother."

Andy laughed out loud.

"I know where to find you," he continued.

Andy turned to face me. "Russell, this is my mate, Mick."

"G'day, my name's Rusty," he said, shaking my hand. There was a certain charisma about him that appealed to me.

"Michael, pleased to meet you."

The conversation eventually went where I feared it would. Andy's forehead creased in the middle. "Talk'n about overcoming life's obstacles. Mick's been through quite a bit." He turned to face me. "Mick was injured on police duty, and a few months ago his house burnt down. Someone burgled the joint and set it alight. Isn't that right Mick?"

I wanted to bury myself then and there. "Yep."

Russell looked me in the eye. "Fire, in our culture, means new beginnings." He guided his hand along the horizon. "Fire removes the old, symbolising a fresh start. Take it as a good sign."

I couldn't help but be drawn to his conviction. A new chapter was to begin.

One Crutch

I began studying Computer Engineering at Box Hill TAFE in 2003. I'm still confused as to why I chose this course; I was never good with computers.

I stepped up my training routine by joining a gym close to home. I attended twice weekly, which included swimming. I sat on the leg extension machine, kicking out my left leg against a kilogram or two of resistance. I looked down to make sure the weight was correct for it felt a lot more like 10 kilograms. I was exhausted after ten repetitions, with the sweat of my t-shirt pressing against my back. I trained my upper torso and arms, reinvigorated with the feeling and memories of youth. In my teens, I trained my body to prove my masculinity and impress women, in gyms that catered to steroid-injected Arnold Schwarzenegger types with bad body odour. The feeling took on a different tone. The focus was on improving my mobility and less on body aesthetics.

I caught people staring at me, observing the way I walked, the look of my atrophied legs. I went from wearing board shorts to wearing track pants in the weights room. I also wore jeans in public on thirty-plus-degree days to avoid uncomfortable stares. The stress levels intensified with people staring at me getting in and out of the pool. I'd focus my attention on the pool attendants assisting me and exchanging smiles with them.

Andrew Duck, the health and fitness coordinator at the gymnasium, added leg presses to my Jane Fonda floor workout. I sat with my feet placed against an inclined metal plate and pushed my quad muscles as hard as I could against a resistance machine. Though I failed to move the plate, I was pleased to see the contractions of my quadriceps, like a car engine when revved up, the mass of the engine block twisted with force on its mounts and springs. As my strength improved I was introduced to the Smith machine. "You're kidding right?" I said to Andrew.

"You can do this exercise," he said with a straight face. He demonstrated the movement of a standard squat with no weight, levelling the bar to where it safely landed. I moved into position under the bar, lifted it, and rotated to unhook the bar as I leaned back into it. I lowered the bar, slightly bending the knees to the point where they felt like buckling under, and back up to the starting position. I felt empowered to continue with the challenge.

I increased my cardiovascular output on the exercise bike and rowing machine. My swimming improved with the hire of a swim coach. The load and expenditure of my output would occasionally invite the hot shooting pain in my legs. It would commence from the hamstrings and down the back of my lower legs and feet. I'd curse, hitting the walls and table. *Is this punishment I get for wanting to walk?* I played "Thunderstruck" in my head each time the pain set in waves, breathing in with its climax, and out with its decline. I continue to suffer the pitchfork treatment whenever I get a cold, feel rundown or suffer urinary tract infections.

After about twelve months my legs gained enough strength for me to walk in public with confidence.

The wheelchair was slowly made redundant. I got rid of it by donating it to the Royal Talbot Rehabilitation Centre in Kew. I could confidently walk to the shopping centre to buy groceries and attend footy matches on weekends.

Over a five-year period, I progressed to walking without the calliper, relying on two crutches alone, then on one crutch out in public. One day, I took this liberty too far: a short walk, without the crutch, from the car to the Post Office, wasn't too difficult – or so I thought. A young man bumped into my side ever so lightly as he rushed out of the Post Office. Like a tower of Jenga blocks, I swayed left to right before collapsing. My keys, envelope and wallet skidded along the footpath. I fell with my hands flat forward to prevent my face from hitting the ground. I felt the heat from the bitumen against my face. A dog nearby, tied to a pole, stared at me with a stretched-out neck, sniffing as his tail wagged. *I know, I must look stupid to you.*

"Sorry, man," the young guy said, grabbing my arm to help me up. "So sorry, man."

"I'm okay, mate," I said, trying to laugh it off. The heat in my cheeks raised a few degrees. "Did you see my pirouette? Looked good, hey?"

I learned to rely on my one crutch at all times when in public.

Lisa

I met Lisa at a birthday party. Her chestnut-coloured eyes and long blonde hair captured my attention. She was as tall as Marta and as pretty as Caroline. About a year-and-a-half into our relationship I developed a gut feeling it wasn't going to last. There developed a communication void between us, silencing our voices and distorting the truth. Lisa's persistent sullen mood after a visit from her mother didn't help; I figured she hadn't favoured me to be her daughter's lover. Lisa shied away whenever I advanced to make love to her. I was unfaithful to her on more than one occasion and felt such remorse for the foolish deeds. My frustration with the failing relationship revealed itself daily.

One day we sat at an outdoor café, feeling the weight of a struggling relationship. My head was filled with disappointment at the lack of interest from Lisa in the idea of seeing a couple's counsellor. Her silence on the subject was irritating me. A couple of guys happened to walk past and almost tripped over my crutch.

"Oh sorry," one said, looking at the crutch. He then turned to me, "What did ya do? Footy injury?"

Typically, I'd ignore the instinct to say, "none of your business," only to divulge the nature of my injury from the car accident. I replied in short, "Mate, I don't wanna talk about it." My expression must've given away a 'fuck off' look for him to recoil. I sensed the end was a matter of days away; my inhibitions were discarded at will.

One day, I walked into the concourse at 101 Collins Street, during the lunch-time rush hour. Workers filed into the elevator ahead of me. I was late for an appointment with my stockbroker. I clunked my way along the marble floor, my sole intention was to catch the lift before the doors shut.

"Come on, hoppity," yelled a man in a business suit, holding the door open. The haughty laughter of his companions sparked my anger.

I quickened my pace to reach the lift in time. "Thanks," I said to him, nodding in acknowledgement with a pressed smile.

He didn't look much older than me. I noticed a businesswoman standing in the corner of the lift clutching her handbag. I gripped the handle of the crutch to steady my stance as the lift ascended. I slowed my breathing and took off my scarf.

"That looks nasty," the man said, staring at my leg. He pressed his spectacles on the bridge of his nose. "How did you injure yourself?"

"I bet you did an ACL playing footy?" said his mate.

"You broke ya leg skiing?" said another.

I zeroed my eyes onto Mr Spectacles. "The Gulf War."

The cabin went silent. Mr Spectacles cleared his throat, staring down at the tip of his shoes.

I continued, "Yeah, '91 was a bad year." I waited until the air had become saturated with discomfort. "Naah, just kidding."

The woman turned to me and smiled.

Lisa accompanied her mother on an overseas trip. She would return in two weeks. The end was nigh, for I sensed her mother would try and talk her into ending our relationship. My feeling proved to be accurate – when Lisa returned, she phoned me. "I need to see you." Her voice was terse and hesitant. We met at my place, and without much discussion about her vacation she proceeded, "I want to break up with you."

I headed out to drink alone, feeling brave and with little care for the consequences.

    I stood tall, all five-foot-seven of me, walking with my chest out among the jungle of hotel patrons. Scotch and Coke was my companion. The bladder needed emptying for my night to continue. There was no disabled toilet, and the cubicles were occupied, so I was forced to step up on the landing of the soaked urinal and lean on the pillar in preparation to self-catheterise. My crutch was set aside next to the washbasin. I pulled out the catheter sleeve from my pocket and smoothed out the kinks. I peeled open the plastic encasing to release the catheter. I held the lining in my left hand as I tried to rip open the lubricant gel between my teeth and right forefinger. The catheter swung left to right as the sachet slipped from my grasp and landed at my feet. "Shit! Fuck!" I stretched as far as my hamstrings allowed, picking up the damp sachet by the fingertips. I made small steps to the basin, washed the sachet under the hot faucet and dried it with a disposable paper towel while the catheter in my left hand swung freely in the air. I went back onto the landing with shaky legs. I ripped the sachet open and lubricated the catheter. The door swung open with the sound of drunken laughter behind me. My heart raced and fingers trembled as the young guys approached close behind.

I lifted my shirt and tried to push the tip of the catheter through the stoma. The boys took up their position at the urinal, and the loudest of them stood next to me. The sweat rested on my brow as I pushed harder, bending the catheter left and right to get the best angle of entry. I could feel his eyes all over me.

"Fuck," I mumbled.

"Hey man… looks like you're in trouble," he said, chuckling.

The smell of alcohol was strong on him. I drew out a long breath before the urine started to flow. I turned to see him staring at the catheter. The flow stalled.

"Shit man… are you in trouble?" he said.

"Fuck." I twisted the catheter around and contracted my abdominal muscles to force the urine to discharge. I turned to him. "What?" My anger was expressed through my voice. "You haven't seen one of these before?"

"Be Strong"

I studied a master's degree in Entrepreneurship and Innovation at Swinburne University in 2008. The three-year course coincided with volunteer work for people with disabilities. Prior to that I had completed a two-year diploma in International Business at the same university, a pathway entry to the master's course. I was interested in pursuing a career in business and investments. I had a taste for the money markets and an interest in helping the marginalised. And though I refused to acknowledge it, I was hell-bent on making Mum and Dad proud of my progression and having them move past the tragedy of the previous years.

I went to visit Mum and Dad one Sunday afternoon. I sat on my favourite chair at the kitchen table with my legs stretched out. "What do you think of my haircut, Dad?" I had cut my long, thick hair short, leaving some length at the top parted to one side.

The delighted look on his face confirmed his approval. "Much better," he said, sipping his espresso.

I lowered my eyelids slightly, enough to capture the Van Gogh-esque blanket of wilting tomatoes and their aroma of near decay. The plants hung on desperately to their wooden stakes; the soil leeched of its nutrients.

"You ok, Michelangelo?" Mum asked.

"Yeah, why?"

"You tired?"

"A little bit," I said with a sigh.

"I know, I can see. Tsk, why you tired?"

"It was a busy week, Mum." I counted one to four fingers, "Uni, physio, gym and *lavoro volontario* (voluntary work)."

"No too much for you, Michal?"

I placed my hands behind my head, "Nah."

"You want a drink or someting to eat?"

"No thanks, Ma."

"What for you work, Michal?" Dad said with a raspy voice. He didn't like the fact I worked without pay.

"Because I like to help people, Dad," I replied.

He shook his head.

I understood his mind. Mum and Dad arrived as migrants from post-war Europe; a pay packet was the reward for hard labour.

"Besides, I'm working with autonomy." *The word autonomy would impress Dad.*

Mum opened the oven door to inspect the rolled braciola. The aroma of roast meat and garlic filled the room. I noticed the left hinge holding the door was wobbly.

"Ma, is the door not closing properly?"

"Tsk, yep," she replied.

"I'll see if I can get a new one for you, Mum."

Her face lit up. "Really? You can find?"

"Yeah, no problem. I can look up on the computer and see a spare one matching the model."

"Please, Michal," she said, clasping her hands like life depended on it.

I helped out with defects around the home at every opportunity: I replaced tap washers, repaired broken rivets from screen door hinges, replaced the washbasin and door locks, repaired faulty power switches and replaced PVC pipes under the laundry sink. Unlike Mirella and Marcello, I had no partner or children. So completing such tasks, though challenging given my unsteady balance, made me feel important. I still felt that, for Mum and Dad to be proud of their son, I had to be useful somehow.

"Michal, I want to ask," Mum interjected.

I knew it would come up.

"Why Leesa leave you?"

The break-up mattered more to Mum than it did to me. I felt relieved the relationship was over, even though I could never have brought it to an end myself. I had this strange feeling, like I had willed the relationship to end. If I were to interrogate myself, I'd reveal an awful truth – I couldn't see myself ever being in love, nor settling for another. I believed I was undeserving of love; I was convinced my life was one of bachelorhood.

"Mum, we were not a good match."

"She never meet someone like you again, I'm sure."

"Mum, it's best this way… Don't worry, I'm ok."

"Tsk tsk," she said, shaking her head. She stared off into the backyard with that familiar frown of hers. I suspected her mind was lost in some god-awful place. It pained me to see her like this.

"Mum, can I please have some tea?"

She broke her silence and let out a deep sigh. "You want teddy bear biscuits wid de tea?"

I chuckled, "Yeah, why not."

She presented me with a torn packet of teddy bears with several of the biscuits missing.

"The kids have been at them, yeah?" I said, laughing.

"Always dey eat de biscuits."

Mum brought out my coffee mug with the police insignia for my tea. The symbol reminded me of Mum and Dad's torment from the accident. *Why this cup out of the many in the cupboard?* Perhaps to them it was symbolic of my survival, or an extension of me to hold close to their hearts. She filled up the kettle with water and waited for it to boil, standing with hands on her cheeks, deep in thought.

I had a sudden epiphany as if an angel tapped me on the shoulder. "That's life, hey Ma?" I said, staring at the teddy bear's face between my fingers. I just had this urge to say the words, "You can never predict what lies ahead. You can have goals and dreams…but life can throw up curve balls." I got carried away, like I was talking to myself. "The car accident changed everything for me. I have this feeling it was meant to be."

"*Cosa hai detto* (What you say), Michael?"

I explained to Mum what I was saying in Itanglish.

"Eh?!" She said in a rising intonation.

I could see she agreed with me.

She added, "Michelangelo, in my country, de people say de life is same when you born under a star. You born under white star… you lucky. You born under black star… you have bad luck."

This was superstition; yet my long-held belief was confirmed. I walked with the dark shadow, my silent companion. I moved to the tune of his beat. I sang the songs of sorrow and danced in the shade of his suffering. I've learned of his trickery and know not to be afraid.

"I know I'm different." I tapped the table with the biscuit. "Mirella and Marcello were born under a white star," I said, smiling.

She approached and held my face with both hands. "I remember you, a boy, you say 'Be strong, Mum.' You remember? I never forget." She kissed my cheek, tears welling in her eyes. "You be strong, Michelangelo. Be happy."

I held my tears in check, feeling the love melt within.

"*Sei sempre stato forte* (You were always strong) Michelangelo, from when you born, and always you be strong," her voice quivered.

I've never forgotten these words. I remind myself of them every day.

Sakura

The year 2013 marked the twentieth anniversary of my car accident. I wanted to get out of the country, to escape the torment of painful memories and experience the wonders of Japan. To visit Taka.

I dialled Taka's phone number.
"*Moshi moshi*," the mature voice answered.
"Hello Taka, this is Michael, Michael from Australia."
"Ooh, hello Michael." He sounded not much different from memory. "How are you?"
"I'm very good, thanks." I hesitated. "I have something to tell you." My mouth began to dry. "I'm coming over to Japan."
"Oh good. When are you coming over?"
"In April."
"You must stay at my home, ok?"
"Thank you, Taka, I will."
"What have you been doing?"
"Lots has happened since I last saw you." I swallowed. "I was involved in a car accident, which left me disabled." From the silence, I wasn't sure he had registered what I said.

"Oh," he said at last

"I was in a wheelchair. Now, I can walk with a crutch. It happened on duty when I was a policeman many years ago."

"Ok." He thought for a moment, then asked about the accident.

I shared some detail, but wanted to move on from that as quickly as I could.

"I'm looking forward to the cherry blossoms in the countryside," I said to change the mood.

"Yeeeah, it's the right time of year." His voice picked up with enthusiasm. "I will meet you at Narita Airport. You will stay at my home."

"Yes, ok. I look forward to seeing you again."

I wrote in my diary:

I always wanted to go to Japan as I firmly believe it will complete the cycle of my tumultuous life. Everything that has gone before me will reach a point of resolution, this is by revisiting the past. The past is of my time with Taka. I believe when I do meet and engage with Taka, it will bring back a sense of self, or at least I think it will.

It was late April when I arrived at Narita Airport. In the exit lounge, I noticed a tall man wearing a coloured, checkered vest over a long-sleeved shirt.

"That's him," I said to myself, walking toward Taka. The baggage handler kept up with my pace. Taka still looked handsome. His familiar face brought back memories. His greying hair was proof of the thirty years since our last encounter.

"Hello, Michael." He extended his hand to shake mine.

"Hello, Taka." A jumble of nerves emerged. "Were you waiting long?"

"No, it's fine," he said, taking the luggage from the porter.

We settled into his Toyota Hybrid. "You mind if I smoke?" Taka said, pulling out a cigarette from his top pocket.

"Not at all." I didn't know he smoked.

We drove along the highway, a wall of time and change between us. There was much catching up to do to re-establish our lost connection. I folded my arms and spoke to him about my years in the police service, the accident, and retirement.

The cigarette between his fingers moved with the steering wheel. The ash fell off as he listened. "When I was young, before teaching you, I worked with the police in Tasmania."

"I didn't know that."

"Yeeeah, I taught at the academy in self-defence. They wanted me to stay, but we moved to Melbourne."

"Ok. Is that when you started teaching us?"

"Yeeah. And I taught the seniors after your class."

"What year did you leave Australia?"

"I think in 1986."

"I remember the night of your farewell," I said, smiling. "And what did you do when you got back to Japan?"

"I became a school teacher."

"Ok." I turned to my left to capture the pink cherry blossoms dotted over the landscape. They looked paler than I had imagined. "Cherry blossoms are out."

"Yeeah, but they flowered early this season."

"They remind me of home. In spring, I'd kick the football alongside the cherry blossoms on the nature strip, knocking off the petals. They'd fall like snowflakes."

We arrived at a small house on top of a hill, the garden decorated with knee-high manicured plants. A gravel path led to the front door, where Hideko stood.

"Hello," she said, bowing her head.

"Haji…memashite," I said, bowing to her. I thought to speak Japanese out of respect and to impress.

"Please come in," Taka instructed.

Hideko provided a chair for me. I sat down and took off my shoes. The crutch rested against the windowpane beside the door. The interior looked familiar: long-stemmed plants in vases, polished wooden floors and clean paper walls. I walked down the hallway in my socks, unaided, moving like a marionette. Taka and Hideko followed behind, carrying my bags. I continued walking with caution, one foot in front of the other.

"What a lovely home."

"Thank you," Hideko replied.

"Please, sit down," Taka said.

We sat at the dining table as Hideko went to the kitchen to prepare tea. "I have a gift for you, Taka." I presented the parcel. He opened the box to find a pair of silver cuff links imprinted with the Australian flag.

"Oh, thank you, thank you!" The delight on his face lifted my spirits. "I need these for my business shirts." He turned and presented them to Hideko.

"I also have a card for you." I handed him the envelope.

"I need my glasses to read," he said, searching for the drawer. "I'm not young anymore," he laughed.

The letter read:

> *Dear Taka,*
>
> *I am pleased to be reunited after years of absence and much has changed since. If I may say so, you are held in great admiration as a teacher, leader and family man by many (…).*
>
> *I am indebted to you for providing the foundations of strength and resolve to see me through years of difficulty, and for this I am grateful. You set the standard of principles that I aspired to hold to myself. I would like to think that I have achieved this. So thank you on behalf of all of us.*
>
> *May our friendship continue in the years to come.*
>
> *Michael*

He placed the card down and removed his glasses, wiping away the tears with a handkerchief. "Thank you, this means a lot to me."

Hideko delivered the green tea and poured each cup, first to Taka and then to me. He spoke to her in Japanese, translating the message on the card. She looked at me with a smile and bowed. Hideko served smoked salmon, miso soup, horseradish salad, seaweed in soy sauce and white rice. The dishes were served in squared earthenware and white bowls. The smell and sight of the dishes brought back memories of the night I dined with his family in Clayton. I was careful with the sliver of wasabi alongside the salmon – I'd learnt my lesson the last time.

Taka retrieved photos from his drawer. "This is you." I was in my judo whites. In one I was receiving a medal, in another I was kneeling on the mat with club members. The memories came to me like it was yesterday and we spoke for some time.

Taka grabbed my shoulder. "Come, I'll show you your bedroom."

I followed him to a steep staircase.

"Your bed is upstairs." He looked at me for confirmation. "Can you walk upstairs?"

I clapped my hands. "Yep, no problem." I held the rails on either side with each step.

Once at the top, I entered the bedroom. The bed rested next to a window overlooking a forest of bamboo stalks in the garden. I watched as a flock of crows launched from the roof of the neighbouring house, flying overhead with their cries. Their sound was different from the crows back home. I stared at the bamboo stalks in the garden, they appeared out of control, like weeds. A glass cabinet with shelves of trophies and mementos stood at the opposite end. I walked up to it for a closer look. I saw the miniature Leaning Tower of Pisa we gave Taka as a parting gift; a surge of warmth filled me.

"Michael," Taka called out. I walked over to the top of the stairs and looked down. "I want to take you to a special place, not far from here."

Taka and I arrived at the entrance of an ancient garden. Greeting us stood a *torii*. Taka bowed in front of the giant gate, and I did likewise. The structure was coloured bright red, with two vertical posts standing about twenty feet apart. The posts were topped by a large beam extending beyond them and curved up at the ends. Beneath this was a straight beam of the same length.

"This is a very old gate, been here for hundreds of years."

I stood marvelling at the structure.

"Come, we'll go to the shrine."

When we reached the Shinto shrine, Taka instructed me how to wash my hands and mouth before entering. The shrine was much like a church, without opulence. I lit an incense stick and watched the end burn, the aromatic smell brought on a calming effect.

"Now, wave your hand to stop the flame."

I did as I was told.

"Now put the stick here," he pointed to a vase containing sand. "Now make a prayer."

I closed my eyes and wished for inner peace and good health.

"We'll go for a walk now, into the forest."

I picked up my crutch to inspect the rubber stop. The coating hadn't broken yet. "Okay, let's go."

"No, I will take you in a wheelchair."

"No, I can walk, no problem."

"No, no, no, I will push you. It is very far."

We hired a wheelchair from the visitor's office, a clunky 1980s hospital chair with old-fashioned hand brakes. He pushed the chariot along the rocky surface, up and downhill. My arse jarred without a cushion. Taka grunted with effort.

"You okay?" he asked.

The heat of embarrassment engulfed me. "Yes, but I feel guilty." I turned around, "I can walk from here, Taka."

"No, no, it's no problem."

We reached our destination. The surroundings were as beautiful as I had imagined. A steady stream poured into a lake, and an arched footbridge harboured water lilies. The tall trees were mirrored in the still water, their dark green leaves delicate like bristles on a paintbrush, a contrast to the hardy gum leaves back home.

"The gods live here." Taka looked around. "If you sit quietly you can hear them." The north wind whistled through the treetops. I gained a spiritual renaissance sitting there at the water's edge. I looked at Taka, seeking clarification. "That's right, they live in the forest, they are good spirits." I closed my eyes and took a deep breath. The cool air enriched my lungs and freed my mind.

Later that evening, I attended a dinner with Taka and his old friend Shoju Matsuzaki. Shoju walked with a limp, though not as pronounced as mine. Sweet and sour sake made for a long and hardy conversation. Taka was our interpreter. Shoju asked about my injury. I told him my story. He nodded his head in acknowledgement, and in return told me of an injury he had obtained from a farming accident. Pointing to his leg, he lifted the bottom of his trousers, revealing deep, hollowed scars and wasted muscles.

"Why, after all these years, did you want to see Taka?" he asked in Japanese.

I took a deep breath, "I looked up to him, he was my teacher."

"*Hai*," he said, nodding.

"I wanted to reconnect with my past. He's an inspiration to me."

"I understand," Shou said, bowing his head. "He's like a father to you?"

"Yes," I said, bowing in return. I became acutely aware of my constant bowing, which made me feel awkward. I wasn't sure whether this was necessary.

The night continued at a karaoke bar, with more friends joining us. Taka's charm appealed to many. He reminded me of Dad in his heyday, striking up a rapport and sharing a belly laugh. Taka grabbed the microphone and sang a ballad. I observed him flirting with the female waiters. I noticed one lady was very fond of him. He wrapped his arm around her waist after she sat on his lap. She, in turn, placed an arm around his shoulder, staring into his eyes. My image of him began to distort. My suspicions were confirmed when he confessed his infidelity. He wasn't proud of it, praising Hideko for being loyal to him. As I sat among the throng of revellers I began to reflect. *He is no different from me. We're both flawed and equally enriched by our personal experiences.*

Shoju's wife arrived, delivering a gift for me, an owl weighing about 5 kilograms, carved from the wood of a rare tree in Hokkaido. The owl represented happiness, good fortune and strength.

"*Arigatō-gozaimasu*", I said, bowing to Shoju.

He bowed in return and hugged me. The hug was unusual, and surprised me.

My two-week holiday came quickly to an end. On my last day, Taka and Hideko prepared a barbeque. Before the guests arrived, I presented Hideko with a bouquet of Japanese flowers. She smiled, turning to Taka with a look of gratitude.

"Thank you," she said in a soft voice. She placed them neatly in a vase on the dining table.

Grilled skewers of chicken and beef were dwarfed in comparison by the beef steaks and sausages of an Aussie barbeque. Taka's children were now adults and with partners.

"You should come and visit Australia when you have the chance, stay at my place," I said.

"We would like to," his daughter said, smiling. "But we need to save money for our wedding."

"I would like to visit one day," said his son.

"You are most welcome." I turned my attention to the expansive backyard. "Look how much bamboo you have growing here, Taka."

"Nooo, don't mention the bamboo." Taka shook his head. "My wife is always on my back to cut it all down."

I turned to see Hideko shaking her head at him, yet she managed to laugh with us.

The next day, Hideko and Taka sat with me in the airport lounge, waiting for the porter to wheel me to the terminal gate. Taka placed his hand on my shoulder and spoke in Japanese to the two porters, who turned to me and bowed. I didn't ask for a translation. I had a good hunch about what had been said, judging by the reaction. One porter wheeled my bags and the other pushed the wheelchair. I turned around, waving goodbye to Hideko and Taka, not knowing when I'd see them again.

Reunion

The Aquinas College thirty-year reunion was held in late November 2015. It would be the first time in decades I would meet with fellow students and long-lost friends. I was told Caroline would be attending. On the weekend of the event, I stayed over at Dad's place, and he drove me to my destination in Ringwood. My right leg was nervously twitching up and down. I'd recently cut my hair to a decent length and I ran my hand through it, dragging it to the side.

I got out of the car and tucked my shirt in. "Thanks, Dad," I said.

"What time do you want me to pick you up?"

I felt like a school kid again. "Dad, it's okay. I'll find my way home."

"Is no problem, I can pick you up."

"Ah, Dad, it will be late. Don't worry, I'll catch a taxi."

"Ok, bye," he said, waving his hand in the air from the driver's seat. He looked like a proud father seeing off his son at a high school graduation. And I felt every bit that young Michael, thirty years ago.

It had been just over a month since we lost Mum to cancer. I could feel her with me, watching my back. She was the sunlight overlooking my shoulder as I walked toward the noisy crowd. I could hear people laughing. I turned around. Dad was parked across the road, watching my every step.

"See ya, Dad," I yelled out.

He drove off slowly, waving goodbye.

I waved back.

"Hiya, Mick," Leanne, one of the organisers, said with arms outstretched, ready to embrace me at the venue entrance. "Come on in. Here," she handed me a card, "a complimentary drink for you."

"Thanks."

I walked through the crowd; familiar faces stared back at me. They knew of my circumstances. DJ was there, standing at the corner bar with his mates, a beer in hand. We locked eyes. The stare felt a lot longer than it was. He turned away. And I turned to smile at the bartender to draw her attention. "Hi, I'll have an Asahi, thanks." I thought about DJ. *Does he want to reach out? Well, he can come up to me if he wants to.*

"Mick," yelled Pete. He approached from the side and embraced me. "You're looking good," he said, patting me on the back.

"G'day, Pete. It's been so long. Good to see you."

"Mickey T," called out Vinnie. "How are ya?" He clinked his beer bottle to mine.

I felt like a new person, empowered in a way. I reflected back on the young Michael, back to being fun and likeable as described by my school reports. I stood tall with youthful vigour. The sickly feeling of vulnerability was absent, I was accepted as an equal among my peers.

As the night wore on, the strength in my legs began to waver. The pain increased with every minute I stood there talking. The seats were all taken. I looked around and saw Caroline, standing next to the disco floor with its multicoloured lights, swaying to the sound of the 1980s. She was alone, watching a group of girls dancing. I walked toward her, the nerves overtook the aching hip and knee. Holding a beer bottle made my walk appear clumsy.

I reached her. "Hi, Caroline."

She turned to me, "Hey, Mick."

I felt as if she'd anticipated my approach. My heart pounded heavily when our eyes met.

"How are you?" Her smile hadn't changed.

"Yeah, I'm good." I took a sip of my beer. "Have you had a chance to dance?"

She brushed her hair back. "No."

I regretted saying this, as the expectation was for me to ask her to dance. "Well, me neither." I spread my arms out and looked down at my legs. I looked up again and met her eyes. "I move like a robot."

"What happened?" The question was delivered as though she knew the answer.

"I had a bad car accident on police duty, in 1993."

"Oh. I'm sorry to hear that Mick."

"Yeah, but I've gotten over the worst of it. I've managed to get back on my feet and walk again."

"Well, by the look of you, you're doing great."

"Thanks."

Awkward silence quickly filled the space between us. She slowly drank from her champagne glass and I likewise from the beer bottle.

"Would you like to dance?" she asked.

"Nah." I recoiled. I would have taken the opportunity if not for the pain, and the embarrassment at knowing my attempt to dance would look like Virgil Tracy from the Thunderbirds. "But I do need to sit down."

"Oh, I'll grab a chair for you."

"Thanks."

I sat on a stool and held my crutch out as if I were holding a royal staff. Caroline stood beside me, sipping from her glass and watching the dancers.

We went into a deep conversation; she told me she had recently separated after years of marriage and was raising two kids on her own.

She turned to me. "What about you Mick? What are you up to these days?"

I hesitated. "I'm writing a memoir."

"Oh, how exciting! What are you writing about?"

"My life, before and after the car accident." I scratched at the label of the bottle. "It's kind of a contrast of identities, so to speak."

"Interesting. Good on you," she said with a smile. "What made you want to write?"

I shrugged my shoulders. "I felt compelled to tell my story."

"Ok. Well, I'd love to read your book when it's finished."

I rolled my eyes, "You'll be waiting a while."

Caroline laughed. "All good things take time, Mick."

I snorted. "Don't I know it."

The next day I reflected on last night's reunion.

I wrote in my diary about the reunion:

> *I believe my decision to attend the reunion was a cry for acceptance, a redemption of self. Had I hung on to this notion after all these years? To reconcile with the past?*
>
> *I attended to seek closure, to cement past hurts (even though the pain lingers in silence, not as strong as it once was).*
>
> *I feel as if I'd moved on from Caroline. I know that will be the last I'll see of her. My feelings for her have moved on. I am content.*
>
> *I moved on from the boy I was to the man I am today. I am Michelangelo.*

Epilogue

If by chance I meet Moyle again, and his heart is genuine, I am willing to talk with him. I want to look him in the eye, tell my story, and listen to what he is willing to share. I like to think I have the strength and wisdom to do so. I am sure we both want a reclamation of peace, for time is short in this life. The reservoir of pain and anger I once harboured is no longer. My memory of the accident will always remain as a stagnant and repugnant friend. The stark revelation is that the ordeal has shaped me into the man I am today. And for this, I am grateful.

About the author

Michael Tarulli served as a police officer with Victoria Police from 1989 to 2000. He suffered traumatic injuries – including a spinal cord injury – from a car accident while on duty in 1993 at Heidelberg, only to return to administrative tasks after intensive rehabilitation.

Since then, he has earned a Master's Degree in Entrepreneurship and Innovation at Swinburne University. He has dedicated his time to volunteering with not-for-profit organisations, and is an advocate for people with disabilities. He featured in the 2024 short film Through These Crossings, a Good Grief Production.

Michael is a passionate outdoor climber in the Blue Mountains and the Grampians.

'You Be Strong…' My Mother Said is Michael's first book.

Acknowledgements

I thank Dr Michael Maloney and Andrew Walsh OAM, who have been the bedrock of my recovery and sureties in my pursuit of self-acceptance. To Chris Haggarty and Wayne Keogh for the support provided to me and my family when needed. I am forever indebted.

To Elizabeth Harris, who encouraged me to write with honesty and bravery. To Kathryn Tafra for bringing out the best in my writing.

To physiotherapists – Gavin Williams, Andrew Duck, Brendan Haslam, and John Contreras – for their tireless work aiding my efforts to walk with strength.

After all these years, I have not forgotten the medical team at Austin Hospital: the ICU trauma surgeons, nurses, spinal ward specialists, and rehabilitation staff. For your dedication, specialist and medical care, I thank you very much.

I acknowledge the Traditional Custodians of the land I live on, the Wurundjeri people of the Kulin Nation. I pay my respects to Elders past, present and emerging.

www.ingramcontent.com/pod-product-compliance
Lightning Source LLC
Chambersburg PA
CBHW061214070526
44584CB00029B/3831